Getting Started with Drupal Commerce

Learn everything you need to know in order to get your first Drupal Commerce website set up and trading

Richard Jones

[PACKT] open source
PUBLISHING   community experience distilled

BIRMINGHAM - MUMBAI

Getting Started with Drupal Commerce

First published: September 2013

Production Reference: 1170913

Published by Packt Publishing Ltd.
Livery Place
35 Livery Street
Birmingham B3 2PB, UK.

ISBN 978-1-78328-023-0

www.packtpub.com

Cover Image by Myles Davidson (myles@i-kos.com)

Credits

Author

Richard Jones

Reviewers

Nick Abbott

Sil Kogelman

Acquisition Editors

Andrew Duckworth

Julian Ursell

Commissioning Editor

Nikhil Chinnari

Technical Editors

Novina Kewalramani

Anita Nayak

Project Coordinator

Akash Poojary

Proofreader

Simran Bhogal

Indexer

Monica Ajmera Mehta

Production Coordinator

Aditi Gajjar

Cover Work

Aditi Gajjar

Foreword

Drupal Commerce is the fastest growing open source solution for building modern e-commerce websites. It extends the popular and proven Drupal CMS, bringing you the best of two worlds: e-commerce and rich, socially enabled content management, all in one package.

Powerful tools require training and skill to use properly, and that's why you need this book. The author carefully sets the stage for a multitude of practical and common e-commerce needs, including a planning template that will help you succeed in e-commerce even before you dive into the details of the software.

Careful planning can uncover many of the issues that a new merchant may overlook, at their own risk. For example, the presentation of products using multiple currencies, sales tax versus VAT, handling of refunds, and compliance issues such as PCI DSS are all important to account for and address.

Drupal Commerce presents a large set of new topics and requires skills that layer on top of the already powerful Drupal software. These include creating products, customizing the cart and checkout processes, configuring taxes, managing orders and shipping, and stimulating sales with discounts and coupons.

Getting Started with Drupal Commerce strikes a nice balance between the conceptual underpinnings of Drupal Commerce and practical guidance, with ongoing examples to create an actual example store. By the end, you have the hands-on experience of actually building something with Drupal Commerce.

Welcome to the world of Drupal Commerce. Happy reading!

Robert Douglass
Director of Product Strategy, Commerce Guys

About the Author

Richard Jones is the Technical Director of i-KOS, a UK-based digital agency, specializing in Drupal and e-commerce. He has been working with the project leads of Drupal Commerce since the early planning stages and maintains a number of contributed modules on `drupal.org` under the username `ikos`.

Since joining i-KOS as Technical Director in 2003, Richard has worked with Managing Director Myles Davidson to build the business from a 3-person web agency into a 20-person e-commerce consultancy powered by Drupal. During that time, he has worked on some of the largest high-profile Drupal Commerce builds to date.

He heads up all Drupal site builds and e-commerce projects at i-KOS. He specializes in Drupal site development, training, and bespoke module development, internet strategy, and e-commerce. He is a prolific Drupal module contributor and regular speaker at UK and international Drupal events.

Outside of the Drupal world, Richard lives in the South coast of England in Hove, with his wife and two young daughters.

I would like to thank the following people for their help and support during the writing of this book:

Nick Abbott of i-KOS, for his characteristic diligence and commitment when working through the first drafts of this book to make it a much more effective training guide.

The entire team at Commerce Guys and all of the other contributors to the Drupal Commerce project for building a set of tools which are so amazing, that I was compelled to write about them!

All of the Drupal Community for introducing me to the world of Open Source and how a software community can really work.

Finally, my wife Elaine, for being a constant support and convincing me to start this project in the first place.

About the Reviewers

Nick Abbott is a full time Drupal Web Development Consultant / Trainer, and Open Source evangelist.

Trained as an Applied Physicist in the mid-1980s, Nick began his teaching career in 1989, and after many years in IT in the independent education sector he moved full time into the commercial web industry in the Autumn of 2008 to focus exclusively on Drupal, and in particular, Drupal Commerce.

As a staunch advocate of Open Source community-driven projects, Nick promotes investment in people, systemization, training, and support over expenditure on software per se.

He currently provides training through i-KOS Digital Services, a London-based Drupal Commerce specialist.

> I would like to thank the author Richard Jones, for all his patience and good humor in putting up with my insistence on attention to fine detail when reviewing this work.

Sil Kogelman is a self-made Dutch entrepreneur with a passion for helping other entrepreneurs with the things that they want to achieve. He loves coming up with solutions that make a project better — practical solutions that bring the project a step closer to its goal. He does this in the fields of digital product creation and marketing.

Sil is known in the Drupal community under his Drupal alias S1L.

Getting to the point of being able to review this book would not be possible without the inspiration I had in my early days of Drupal. The Drupal Community by itself inspires me, and Nate Haugh and Ryan Szrama inspire and impress me the most.

I would also like to thank my girlfriend Nadine Atmo for being so supportive of me. You rock my world honey. I love you.

www.PacktPub.com

Support files, eBooks, discount offers and more

You might want to visit www.PacktPub.com for support files and downloads related to your book.

Did you know that Packt offers eBook versions of every book published, with PDF and ePub files available? You can upgrade to the eBook version at www.PacktPub.com and as a print book customer, you are entitled to a discount on the eBook copy. Get in touch with us at service@packtpub.com for more details.

At www.PacktPub.com, you can also read a collection of free technical articles, sign up for a range of free newsletters and receive exclusive discounts and offers on Packt books and eBooks.

http://PacktLib.PacktPub.com

Do you need instant solutions to your IT questions? PacktLib is Packt's online digital book library. Here, you can access, read and search across Packt's entire library of books.

Why Subscribe?

- Fully searchable across every book published by Packt
- Copy and paste, print and bookmark content
- On demand and accessible via web browser

Free Access for Packt account holders

If you have an account with Packt at www.PacktPub.com, you can use this to access PacktLib today and view nine entirely free books. Simply use your login credentials for immediate access.

Table of Contents

Preface

Getting Started with Drupal Commerce is an introductory guide to the Commerce suite of modules for Drupal 7. You will be guided through the basic concepts needed to understand how the Commerce framework is designed, by reference to a real life case study site. At the end of the book, you will be prepared to set up your own store and understand the potential of Drupal Commerce as a framework.

What this book covers

Chapter 1, Introducing Key Concepts, takes you through the basic terminology used in Drupal Commerce and how the key components work together.

Chapter 2, Installing Drupal Commerce, explains how to add Drupal Commerce to a working Drupal 7 installation.

Chapter 3, Planning Your Store, deals with checklists and preparation for your e-commerce store, ensuring you have considered the business requirements before you start using the software.

Chapter 4, Products, shows you how to set up your product catalogue and display pages.

Chapter 5, Shopping Cart, shows you how to give the customer the ability to select products from your store for purchase.

Chapter 6, Checkout, explains how to take the customer through the checkout process for payment and confirmation.

Chapter 7, Shipping, explains how to add the ability for the customer to select a shipping address and method for their order.

Chapter 8, Tax, shows you how to define and configure sales tax and VAT for your store.

Chapter 9, Managing Orders, introduces backoffice screens to allow you to process orders as they come in.

Chapter 10, Discounts and Coupons, shows you how to set up some rules based on discounts for your products.

Chapter 11, Extending Commerce, is not present in the book but is available as a free download from the following link: `http://www.packtpub.com/sites/default/files/downloads/0230OS_11_Extending Commerce.pdf`.

What you need for this book

All you need is a working installation of Drupal 7. We recommend using a local development environment, such as Acquia Dev Desktop available at `https://www.acquia.com/downloads`.

Drupal Commerce works in any modern browser. You will not need to edit any PHP code to complete the chapters in this book.

Who this book is for

You do not need any previous experience of Drupal 7 in order to complete the chapters of this book, but a working knowledge of Drupal will be useful.

The book is intended for e-commerce store owners and developers who are looking to set up an e-commerce experience.

Conventions

In this book, you will find a number of styles of text that distinguish between different kinds of information. Here are some examples of these styles, and an explanation of their meaning.

Code words in text, database table names, folder names, filenames, file extensions, pathnames, dummy URLs, user input, and Twitter handles are shown as follows: "Uncompress the downloaded file to `Sites` in your `User` folder."

New terms and **important words** are shown in bold. Words that you see on the screen, in menus, or dialog boxes for example, appear in the text like this: "Click on the **Sites** tab, as shown in the following screenshot."

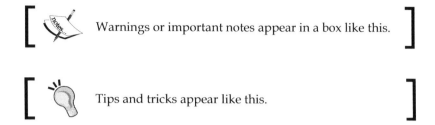

Warnings or important notes appear in a box like this.

Tips and tricks appear like this.

Reader feedback

Feedback from our readers is always welcome. Let us know what you think about this book—what you liked or may have disliked. Reader feedback is important for us to develop titles that you really get the most out of.

To send us general feedback, simply send an e-mail to feedback@packtpub.com, and mention the book title via the subject of your message.

If there is a topic that you have expertise in and you are interested in either writing or contributing to a book, see our author guide on www.packtpub.com/authors.

Customer support

Now that you are the proud owner of a Packt book, we have a number of things to help you to get the most from your purchase.

Downloading the example code

You can download the example code files for all Packt books you have purchased from your account at http://www.packtpub.com. If you purchased this book elsewhere, you can visit http://www.packtpub.com/support and register to have the files e-mailed directly to you.

Errata

Although we have taken every care to ensure the accuracy of our content, mistakes do happen. If you find a mistake in one of our books—maybe a mistake in the text or the code—we would be grateful if you would report this to us. By doing so, you can save other readers from frustration and help us improve subsequent versions of this book. If you find any errata, please report them by visiting http://www.packtpub.com/submit-errata, selecting your book, clicking on the **errata submission form** link, and entering the details of your errata. Once your errata are verified, your submission will be accepted and the errata will be uploaded on our website, or added to any list of existing errata, under the Errata section of that title. Any existing errata can be viewed by selecting your title from http://www.packtpub.com/support.

Piracy

Piracy of copyright material on the Internet is an ongoing problem across all media. At Packt, we take the protection of our copyright and licenses very seriously. If you come across any illegal copies of our works, in any form, on the Internet, please provide us with the location address or website name immediately so that we can pursue a remedy.

Please contact us at copyright@packtpub.com with a link to the suspected pirated material.

We appreciate your help in protecting our authors, and our ability to bring you valuable content.

Questions

You can contact us at questions@packtpub.com if you are having a problem with any aspect of the book, and we will do our best to address it.

1

Introducing Key Concepts

This chapter introduces Drupal and Drupal Commerce while explaining the goals of the system:

- Introduction to the Drupal Commerce project and its origins
- The framework concept of Drupal Commerce and how this allows you to build any type of e-commerce experience on top of Drupal
- Examples of the types of stores that can be created using Drupal Commerce

An introduction to Drupal Commerce

Drupal Commerce is a suite of modules written for Drupal 7 that enable you to create flexible, full-featured e-commerce sites. It is best described as an e-commerce framework as opposed to an out of the box shopping cart system. At the time of writing, Drupal 8 had not been released, but there is a roadmap available for the release of Commerce for Drupal 8 (`http://www.drupalcommerce.org/roadmap`).

Like Drupal itself, the Commerce framework components provided can be combined and extended to create any kind of e-commerce site, so you are not restrained by the default capabilities of the system.

The project is headed by Ryan Szrama of Commerce Guys; a French/American company dedicated to developing and supporting the Drupal Commerce platform. Drupal Commerce 1.0 was officially launched at DrupalCon London in 2011.

Unlike some other open source platforms, there are no premium or paid versions of Drupal Commerce. What you download from `http://www.drupal.org/project/commerce` is everything you need to get started.

The core Drupal Commerce download consists of the following modules:

- Commerce (core module)
- Cart
- Checkout
- Customer
- Line item
- Order
- Payment
- Price
- Product
- Product pricing
- Product reference
- Tax

The system was designed using a small core philosophy: the core modules only contain the components considered essential for every e-commerce site. For example, the shipping functionality is not included in core since it isn't necessary that every system has physical goods to ship. The rationale behind the system is to make no assumptions about the business logic of the system being built—rather it provides an extensible framework for development.

There are many modules available on `Drupal.org` that extend Drupal Commerce for different use cases. We will discuss some of them in this book.

Drupal Commerce exceeded 230,000 downloads in July 2013 and is used to power some high-profile and high-volume websites.

Products that can be sold

Due to its nature as a flexible framework, Drupal Commerce is well suited to create many types of e-commerce experiences, from simple to complex.

Some examples include:

- Physical products
- Gifts
- Books and CDs
- Digital downloads

- Software
- Music
- Subscriptions
- Magazines
- Events and tickets
- Theatres
- Conferences
- Paid content access
- Paywall access to content
- Bespoke products
- Customizable products
- Greetings cards

You could also use the system to design a backend order processing system for a single-page promotional site. With a good understanding of the system, the possibilities are limitless.

Key terminology

Before starting out with your Drupal Commerce build, it's important to understand the key terminology used to describe the different components of the system.

Drupal 7 introduced the concept of an **Entity** as a way to represent a discrete piece of content. In Drupal Core, a **User** and a **Node** are entities and any entity can be extended using **Fields**. A Field is used to represent an aspect of content such as the title, username, or description. Drupal Commerce defines a number of new Entity types that are used as the building blocks of the system.

The Product module

A product represents an item for sale on your website. It can be a physical product such as a book, or a virtual product, such as a digital download or event. You can add fields to your product to represent different elements—for example color, size or, in the case of an event, a date.

You can also define multiple types of products each with different fields to best categorize the products within your store.

The Order module (commerce_order)

In Drupal Commerce, the order entity is used to represent a customer order in any state. The moment the customer adds something to their shopping cart, a new order is created. As with products, an order can be extended with different fields to hold custom information about an order.

You can define multiple order types if your business requires a distinction between them—for example, a stock order and a subscription order.

The Line item module (commerce_line_item)

An order is made up of one or more Line items. A line item associates a product with an order.

By default, a line item will only contain a product reference (that is, a pointer to an actual product), and quantity. Line items can be extended with additional fields allowing you to collect more specific information. You could extend this, for example, to create a personalized gift message for an order line.

You can define multiple line item types, for example, for customizable and non-customizable products.

The Customer profile module (commerce_profile)

A customer profile is used to store the personal details of your customer. An order will generally be associated with one or more Customer profiles—typically one for the invoice address and one for the shipping address.

You can extend the customer profile with additional fields if you want to collect more information from the customer. Typical uses for this might include a telephone number, special delivery instructions, and so on.

You can define different Customer profile types allowing you to collect different information for billing and shipping, for example.

The Payment transaction module (commerce_payment_transaction)

If you have integrated your store with a payment gateway, the gateway module will create one or more payment transactions and associate them with your order. The contents of these vary depending on the payment gateway implementation, but typically will include the payment details and response from the card payment provider to the request for payment.

We will discuss how to use these concepts in a lot more detail in *Chapter 3, Planning Your Store*.

Prerequisites and dependencies

Drupal Commerce makes use of several other key Drupal contributed modules. Some of them are listed and explained in the coming sections as follows:

The Views module

The Views module (http://drupal.org/project/views) is used extensively throughout Drupal Commerce for almost all the administration screens and shopping cart / checkout. The fact that almost everything in Drupal Commerce is powered by Views makes it very easy to modify the shopping experience for both the customer and store owner without the need for coding.

The Rules module

The Rules module (http://drupal.org/project/rules) is used in many contexts throughout Drupal Commerce including for the calculation of prices and taxes. Rules is a very flexible and extensible system and provides many options for implementing the rules of your business.

The Entity module

The Entity module (http://drupal.org/project/entity) allows much greater access to the entity data that makes up the Commerce system. This will be of great benefit if you start to develop more comprehensive sites using Rules and particularly if you plan to write your own Drupal Commerce modules.

The Address Field module

Instead of defining its own Address field standard, Drupal Commerce utilizes the Address Field module (http://drupal.org/project/addressfield), which uses international standard address formats (xNAL) to ensure that all countries' address standards are supported.

The Chaos Tools module

The **Chaos Tools** (**Ctools**) module (http://drupal.org/project/ctools) is a utility module that allows Drupal Commerce to implement a common pluggable architecture.

The Token module

The Token module (http://drupal.org/project/token) provides text placeholders that represent (and are expanded into) entity properties or fields depending on the context of where the token is used. For example, when visiting a user's profile page, the token [user], would represent the user's **unique ID** (**uid**) and within the context of an actual item of content such as a page, [author] might expand to the author of the post, that is also the uid property of the item of content.

The Pathauto module

The Pathauto module (http://drupal.org/project/pathauto) automatically generates URL/path aliases for various kinds of content (nodes, taxonomy terms, and users) without requiring the user to manually specify the path alias.

Customizing and extending

One of the most exciting aspects of working with Drupal is the fact that you can extend and customize the system to your own requirements. You can either create your own custom modules or there are hundreds of free add-on modules on the drupal.org website. So if you want to have a shipping calculation that works with your product set, or you need to get your data from a legacy database in your company, you are not limited by the initial capabilities of the software. As it is open source, you are not locked into using a proprietary vendor to make changes—you can do it yourself!

You can also find a more curated list of Drupal Commerce specific modules at drupalcommerce.org.

Summary

By the end of this chapter, the reader should have an understanding of the potential of Drupal Commerce and how it came about. They should also understand the motivation of the developers.

2

2
Installing Drupal Commerce

Drupal Commerce was developed for Drupal 7, so before you start, you will need a working Drupal 7 installation.

At the time of writing, the current release of Drupal 7 is 7.23, which can be downloaded from `http://drupal.org/project/drupal`.

System requirements

In order to run Drupal Commerce, you will need a server with the following downloads:

- Web server, namely Apache, Nginx, or Microsoft IIS
- PHP 5.2.5, or higher (5.3 recommended)
- MySQL 5.0.15, or higher with PDO

More details can be found on the Drupal website: `http://drupal.org/requirements`

 While you can use different web servers and databases to run Drupal, the screenshots and examples in this book assume an Apache based web server running on Mac OS X with MySQL.

If you do not have access to a web server, you can download the free Acquia Dev Desktop package, which contains everything you need for a local Drupal development stack in a single cross-platform download. As development is much easier on a local basis, this book assumes that you are using Acquia Dev Desktop, and the rest of this chapter explains how to get your Drupal Commerce store up and running in a local environment. The instructions here also assume that you are using Mac OS X, but will work equally well in Windows.

Downloading Acquia Dev Desktop

If you have a working server environment that has the minimum requirements for running Drupal, you can skip straight to the *Setting up a new Drupal site* section.

Acquia Dev Desktop is a cross-platform **Apache**, **MySQL**, **PHP** (**AMP**) stack that contains everything you need for a local Drupal environment on both Windows and Mac OS X, which is available at `http://acquia.com/downloads`.

Once the file is downloaded, run the installer.

Accept all of the defaults and enter your credentials for accessing your new site. The Dev Desktop application will be installed in your applications folder.

When the application is running, a control panel will be visible, as shown in the following screenshot:

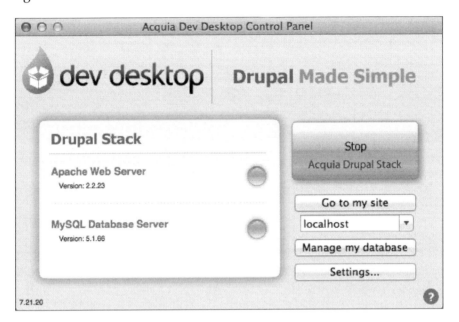

Open the following URL in your web browser:

`http://localhost:8082`

 The Acquia Dev Desktop package installs a configured Drupal profile, specifically for use with the Acquia cloud hosting services.

You will see a default Drupal installation as shown in the following screenshot:

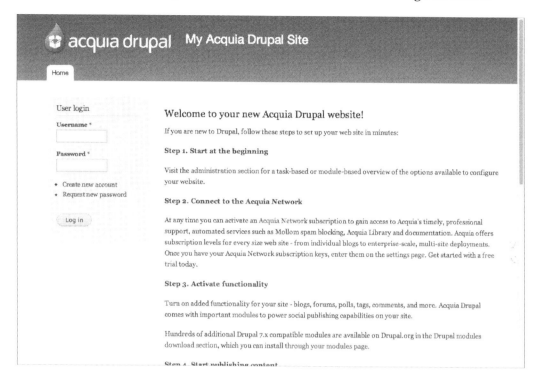

Setting up a new Drupal site

For the purposes of demonstration in this book, we do not need the extra Acquia modules active. Instead, we want a clean Drupal install with Drupal Commerce, so we will now set up a new website.

You can download and install a kickstart version of Drupal Commerce which will set up a number of defaults and immediately give you a demonstration store to experiment with. However, this book is intended to take you step-by-step building on your understanding in each chapter. Download Kickstart from `http://www.drupal.org/project/ commerce_kickstart`.

The following are the steps for setting up a new Drupal site:

1. Download the latest version of Drupal 7 from the `http://drupal.org/` `project/drupal` link as shown in the following screenshot:

2. Uncompress the downloaded file to `Sites` in your `User` folder.

 We suggest renaming the uncompressed folder to simply `drupal` in place of the downloaded version's name of `drupal-7.xx`. This is a convention rather than necessity, but will simplify future upgrades when the core version of Drupal changes.

3. Go back to the Dev Desktop control panel and click on **Settings...**.

4. Click on the **Sites** tab, as shown in the following screenshot:

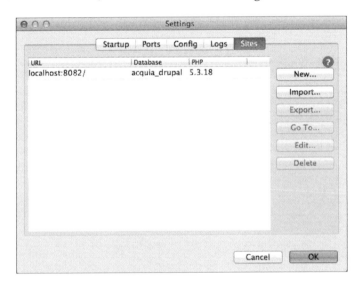

5. Click on the **Import...** button.

6. In the **Import site** screen, set the **Site path** to recently uncompressed and renamed `drupal` folder.

7. The **Subsite** field will show `default` as the only option.

8. Under **Database**, select **Create new database** and give it a suitable name.

9. Enter a new subdomain and then click on **Import**, as shown in the following screenshot:

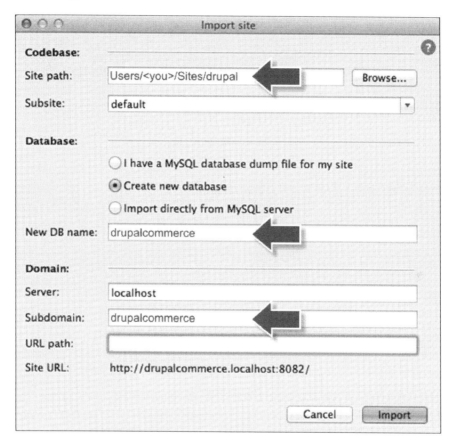

10. Your default browser will open on the Drupal installation page.

11. Select the **Standard** profile, then click on **Save and continue**.

12. Select **English** and click on **Save and continue**.

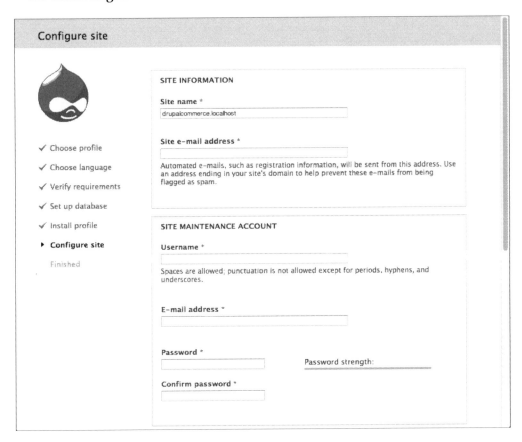

13. When the install process has completed, you will be presented with the **Configure Site** screen, as shown in the previous screenshot.

14. Enter a valid site e-mail address, username, and password.

15. Scroll down and complete the last two sections as appropriate for your region.

16. It is always recommended to select **Check for updates automatically**.

17. Click on **Save and continue**. When this is complete, clicking on the **Visit your new site** link will take you to the home page.

Setting your memory limit

Drupal Commerce requires quite a few additional modules in order to operate. It is advised that you increase the maximum memory limit available to the Drupal site by editing the `sites/drupalcommerce.localhost/settings.php` file.

At the bottom of the file add the following code line:

```
ini_set('memory_limit', '128M');
```

Enabling Drupal Commerce modules

Now that you have a working Drupal installation, we can install the Drupal Commerce modules and dependencies.

Contributed modules should be placed in the `sites/all/modules/contrib` folder.

Download the following modules and unzip them into the `sites/all/modules/contrib` folder:

- `http://drupal.org/project/commerce`
- `http://drupal.org/project/rules`
- `http://drupal.org/project/views`
- `http://drupal.org/project/entity`
- `http://drupal.org/project/addressfield`
- `http://drupal.org/project/ctools`
- `http://drupal.org/project/token`

Your folder should now look like the following screenshot:

Next, go to the modules screen available at `http://drupalcommerce.localhost:8082/#overlay=admin/modules` link.

Drupal Commerce and its dependencies are made up of a large number of modules.

Rather than enable them all right now, we will enable them gradually in the forthcoming chapters, so as to help introduce the functionality provided by each one in turn.

To start with, enable the following module from the **Chaos Tools Suite** package:

- Chaos tools

Next, enable the following modules from the **Commerce** package:

- Cart
- Checkout
- Commerce
- Commerce UI
- Customer
- Line Item
- Order
- Price
- Product
- Product UI
- Product Pricing
- Product Reference

Enable the following module from the **Fields** package:

- Address Field

Enable the following modules from the **Other** package:

- Entity API
- Entity tokens
- Token

Enable the following modules from the **Rules** package:

- Rules
- Rules UI

Enable the following modules from the **Views** package:

- Views
- View UI

Finally, we probably don't want the **Drupal Comment** feature active, so disable that module now.

Summary

In this chapter, we have installed Drupal using Acquia Dev Desktop and enabled all of the required modules for Drupal Commerce.

You now have everything that you need to get started with your Drupal Commerce site.

3
Planning Your Store

Drupal Commerce is an e-commerce framework and so there are often many ways you can meet the business requirements of your e-store. Therefore careful planning is essential. You will save yourself a great deal of time, effort, and frustration if you focus on the details in this chapter before you start building your website.

As with most web projects, the biggest issues you encounter are the ones that no one has thought of, but are obvious in hindsight. The following pages contain checklists of questions to consider when working with the business stakeholders of your new website.

Defining the catalogue

The type of products you are selling will determine the structure of your store. Different types of products will have different requirements in terms of the information presented to the customer, and the data that you will need to collect in order to fulfill an order.

Base product definition

Every product needs to have the following fields which are added by default:

- Title
- Stock Keeping Unit (SKU)
- Price (in the default store currency)
- Status (a flag indicating if the product is live on the store)

This is the minimum you need to define a product in Drupal Commerce—everything else is customized for your store. You can define multiple **Product Types (Product Entity Bundles)**, which can contain different fields depending on your requirements.

Physical products

If you are dealing with physical products, such as books, CDs, or widgets, you may want to consider these additional fields:

- Product images
- Description
- Size
- Weight
- Artist/Designer/Author
- Color

 You may want to consider setting up multiple Product Types for your store. For example, if you are selling CDs, you may want to have a field for `Artist` which would not be relevant for a T-shirt (where `designer` may be a more appropriate field).

Whenever you imagine having distinct pieces of data available, adding them as individual fields is well worth doing at the planning stage so that you can use them for detailed searching and filtering later.

Digital downloads

If you are selling a digital product such as music or e-books, you will need additional fields to contain the actual downloadable file. You may also want to consider including:

- Cover image
- Description
- Author/Artist
- Publication date
- Permitted number of downloads

Tickets

Selling tickets is a slightly more complex scenario since there is usually a related event associated with the product. You may want to consider including:

- Related event (which would include date, venue, and so on)
- Ticket Type / Level / Seat Type

Content access and subscriptions

Selling content access and subscriptions through Drupal Commerce usually requires associating the product with a Drupal role. The customer is buying membership of the role which in turn allows them to see content that would usually be restricted. You may want to consider including:

- Associated role(s)
- Duration of membership
- Initial cost (for example, first month free)
- Renewal cost (for example, £10/month)

Customizing products

The next consideration is whether products can be customized at the point of purchase. Some common examples of this are:

- Specifying size
- Specifying color
- Adding a personal message (for example, embossing)
- Selecting a specific seat (in the event example)
- Selecting a subscription duration
- Specifying language version of an e-book
- Gift wrapping or gift messaging

It is important to understand what additional user input you will need from the customer to fulfill the order over and above the SKU and quantity.

When looking at these options, also consider whether the price changes depending on the options that the customer selects. For example:

- Larger sizes cost more than smaller sizes
- Premium for "red" color choice
- Extra cost for adding an embossed message
- Different pricing for different seating levels
- Monthly subscription is cheaper if you commit to a longer duration

Classifying products

Now that you have defined your Product Types, the next step is to consider the classification of products using Drupal's in-built Taxonomy system.

A basic store will usually have a `catalog` taxonomy vocabulary where you can allocate a product to one or more catalog sections, such as books, CDs, clothing, and so on. The taxonomy can also be hierarchical, however, individual vocabularies for the classification of your products is often more workable, especially when providing the customer with a faceted search or filtering facility later.

The following are examples of common taxonomy vocabulary:

- Author/Artist/Designer
- Color
- Size
- Genre
- Manufacturer/Brand

 It is considered best practice to define a taxonomy vocabulary rather than have a simple free text field. This provides consistency during data entry. For example, a free text field for size may end up being populated with S, Small, Sm, all meaning the same thing. A dropdown taxonomy selector would ensure that the value entered was the same for every product. Do not be tempted to use List type fields to provide dropdown menus of choices. List fields are necessarily the reserve of the developer and using them excludes the less technical site owner or administrator from managing them.

Pricing

Drupal Commerce has a powerful pricing engine, which calculates the actual selling price for the customer, depending on one or more predefined rules. This gives enormous flexibility in planning your pricing strategy.

Currency

Drupal Commerce allows you to specify a default currency for the store, but also allows you to enter multiple price fields or calculate a different price based on other criteria, such as the preferred currency of the customer.

If you are going to offer multiple currencies, you need to consider how the currency exchange will work; do you want to enter a set price for each product and currency you offer, or a base price in the default currency and calculate the other currencies based on a conversion rate?

If you use a conversion rate, how often is it updated?

Variable pricing

Prices do not have to be fixed. Consider scenarios where the prices for your store will vary over time, or situations based on other factors such as volume-based discounts.

Will some preferred customers get a special price deal on one or more products?

Customers

You cannot complete an order without a customer and it is important to consider all of their needs during the planning process.

By default, a customer profile in Drupal Commerce contains an address type field which works to the **Name and Address Standard (xNAL)** format, collecting international addresses in a standard way. However, you may want to extend this profile type to collect more information about the customer. For example:

- Telephone number
- Delivery instructions
- E-mail opt-in permission

Do any of the following apply?

- Is the store open to public or open by invitation only?
- Do customers have to register before they can purchase?
- Do customers have to enter an e-mail address in order to purchase?
- Is there a geographical limit to where products can be sold/shipped?
- Can a customer access their account online?
- Can a customer cancel an order once it is placed? What are the time limits on this?
- Can a customer track the progress of their order?

Taxes

Many stores are subject to Sales tax or **Value Added Tax (VAT)** on products sold. However, these taxes often vary depending on the type of product sold and the final destination of the physical goods.

During your planning you should consider the following:

- What are the sales tax / VAT rules for the store?
- Are there different tax rules depending on the shipping destination?
- Are there different tax rules depending on the type of product?

If you are in a situation where different types of products in your store will incur different rates of taxes, then it is a very good idea to set up different Product Types so that it's easy to distinguish between them. For example, in the UK, physical books are zero rated for VAT, whereas, the same book in digital format will have 20% VAT added.

Payments

Drupal Commerce can connect to many different payment gateways in order create a transaction for an order. While many of the popular payment gateways, such as PayPal and Sage Pay, have fully functional payment gateway modules on `Drupal. org`, it's worth checking if the one you want is available because creating a new one is no small undertaking.

The following should also be considered:

- Is there a minimum spend limit?
- Will there be multiple payment options?
- Are there surcharges for certain payment types?
- Will there be account customers that do not have to enter a payment card?
- How will a customer be refunded if they cancel or return their order?

Shipping

Not every product will require shipping support, but for physical products, shipping can be a complex area. Even a simple product store can have complex shipping costs based on factors such as weight, destination, total spend, and special offers.

Ensure the following points are considered during your planning:

- Is shipping required?
- How is the cost calculated? By value/weight/destination?
- Are there geographical restrictions?
- Is express delivery an option?
- Can the customer track their order?

Stock

With physical products and some virtual products such as event tickets, stock control may be a requirement. Stock control is a complex area and beyond the scope of this book, but the following questions will help uncover the requirements:

- Are stock levels managed in another system, for example, MRP?
- If the business has other sales channels, is there dedicated stock for the online store?
- When should stock levels be updated (at the point of adding to the cart or at the point of completing the order)?
- How long should stock be reserved?
- What happens when a product is out of stock?
- Can a customer order an out-of-stock product (back order)?
- What happens if a product goes out of stock during the customer checkout process?
- If stock is controlled by an external system, how often should stock levels be updated in the e-store?

Legal compliance

It is important to understand the legal requirements of the country where you operate your store. It is beyond the scope of this book to detail the legal requirements of every country, but some examples of e-commerce regulation that you should research and understand are included here:

- PCI-DSS Compliance — Worldwide
- The Privacy and Electronic Communications (EC Directive) (also known as the EU cookie law) — European Union
- Distance Selling Regulations — UK

Customer communication

Once the customer has placed their order, how much communication will there be? A standard expectation of the customer will be to receive a notification that their order has been placed, but how much information should that e-mail contain?

- Should the e-mail be plain text or graphical?
- Does the customer receive an additional e-mail when the order is shipped?
- If the product has a long lead time, should the customer receive interim updates?
- What communication should take place if a customer cancels their order?

Back office

In order for the store to run efficiently, it is important to consider the requirements of the back office system. This will often be managed by a different group of people to those specifying the e-store. Identify the different types of users involved in the order fulfillment process. These roles may include:

- Sales order processing
- Warehouse and order handling
- Customer service for order enquiries
- Product managers

These roles may all have different information available to them when trying to locate the order or product they need, so it's important for the interface to cater to different scenarios:

- Does the website need to integrate with a third-party system for management of orders?
- How are order status codes updated on the website so that customers can track progress? In a batch, manually or automatically?

User experience

How will the customer find the product that they are looking for?

- Well-structured navigation?
- Search by SKU?
- Free text search?
- Faceted search?

The source of product data

When you are creating a store with more than a trivial number of products, you will probably want to work on a method of mass importing the product data.

Find out where the product data will be coming from, and in what format it will be delivered. You may want to define your Product Types taking into account the format of the data coming in—especially if the incoming data format is fixed.

You may also want to define different methods of importing taxonomy terms from the supplied data.

Summary

Once you have gone through all of these checklists with the business stakeholders, you should have enough information to start your Drupal Commerce build. Drupal Commerce is very flexible, but it is crucial that you understand the outcome that you are trying to achieve before you start installing modules and setting up Product Types.

4
Products

The remaining chapters of this book will lead you through the creation of an example store based on a real-life scenario. As we progress, we will build up the functionality of the store and discuss each key concept in turn. Our demonstration site is a UK-based company selling wholesale coffee and tea-related wares.

Setting up the store currency

Before we start setting up our products, we should first set the default currency and any other currencies that we want to make available.

Visit the store page and configure. Click on **Currency settings** to set the **Default store currency** field to **GBP - British Pounds Sterling - £**.

Since we are selling only in the UK, we should, for completeness, disable the out-of-the-box default currency of USD too.

Using our clean installation from *Chapter 2*, *Installing Drupal Commerce*, we are ready to start defining our products.

Planning our products

The majority of the products on the site are bags of coffee beans and tea leaves in various packaging formats.

Thus, we can fully define a sellable product with the following fields:

- Title
- Stock Keeping Unit
- Description
- Price

- Image
- Pack size
- Physical weight

Product entities and product displays

One of biggest points of confusion for those new to Drupal Commerce is the concept of working with product entities and associated product displays.

I will now attempt to explain the reasoning behind this concept, and I will then introduce you to some extra helper modules that make life significantly easier when it comes to working with the model.

With a base Commerce installation, when you create your products, you do not actually have an automatic way to display them on the website which initially seems rather strange.

The reason is that sellable products are actually examples (instances, if you will), of specialized product entities as provided by the Commerce product module, and as such are not viewable nodes in the conventional sense.

In order to display a product on the website, a traditional Drupal node must be associated with one or more actual physical products using a product reference field. It is via the associated node that the customer actually views the product rather than viewing the product entity itself.

At first, this seems confusing; almost as if you have to add your product data twice. However, it is actually a very logical framework decision, as will become clear.

Variations on a theme

Sellable products very often have multiple variations, for example size or color.

Let's look at a simple example of a t-shirt—if you have a design in three sizes and three colors, that is a total of nine physical products.

From a browsing perspective

If a customer is browsing the site, it's more likely that you will want to show them a single representative product rather than nine that look almost identical. That is to say, when the customers visit the t-shirts page, they will expect to see one t-shirt style available in a variety of colors and sizes. Moreover, they will expect to be able to navigate through the various size or color combinations via widgets, such as drop-down menus.

Once again, in the Commerce model, the browsable shop window items are just good old fashioned nodes (product displays) with links to one or more actual products.

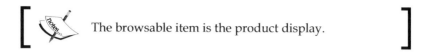

> The browsable item is the product display.

From a buying perspective

When a customer actually buys the product, you, the seller, need to know exactly which one they've ordered. It's more than likely that you will want to control stock of each color and size variation individually, therefore each different size or color must be a distinct product with a unique **Stock Keeping Unit**.

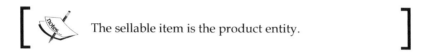

> The sellable item is the product entity.

Managing the product entity or product display marriages

So, now that we are clear (I hope) about the product/product display concept that Commerce employs out of the box, we will now get you going with a few extras to help make the management of the marriage a lot easier.

The Commerce Backoffice module, along with a small collection of other than helper modules, hides a lot of the complexity away with an improved user interface. Before we start, we need to download and install some helper modules which make setting up the store much easier.

Download the following modules:

- `http://drupal.org/project/commerce_backoffice`
- `http://drupal.org/project/views_bulk_operations`
- `http://drupal.org/project/views_megarow`
- `http://drupal.org/project/inline_entity_form`

Some of these downloads contain more than one module, so enable the following modules before continuing:

- Commerce Backoffice (Commerce package)
- Commerce Backoffice (Product package)

The others are dependencies and so will be enabled automatically.

It's a good job that we haven't yet started interacting with Commerce to manage our products, since activating these modules makes some fairly significant alterations to both the product UI and actual terminology.

Terminology changes

By enabling the Commerce Backoffice module, we trigger some terminology changes which make the concepts described in this chapter much easier to comprehend. Firstly, what we formerly referred to as product displays, we'll now call product display nodes, or better still just products.

Secondly, what we formerly referred to as products, we'll now refer to as product variations.

I'm sure you'll agree that this new terminology makes good sense and is easier to relate to than the out-of-the-box defaults.

Ensuring unique product titles

Since we are going to be using the combination of modules detailed earlier, aside from the SKU, we will need at least one other field to be a **Taxonomy** reference field that can be used to distinguish one product variation from another uniquely.

It makes a lot of sense to use the **Pack size** field for this purpose because the Inline Entity Form module can be configured to shape the product variations' titles using any specially-denoted taxonomy fields. See later for details as and when we add this particular field, but for now, let's get set up for the job by creating a Taxonomy vocabulary which contains all of the possible pack sizes. For our simple example of a products list, we will use the following pack sizes:

- Barrel
- Caddy
- Foil wrapped
- Sample

Thus, create a new Taxonomy vocabulary, called `Pack size` and add the terms shown in the following screenshot:

NAME	OPERATIONS
⊹ Barrel	edit
⊹ Caddy	edit
⊹ Foil wrapped	edit
⊹ Sample	edit

Defining a new product variation type

The following are the steps to define a new product variation type:

1. Click on **Store** in the main toolbar.

2. Click on **Configuration**.

3. Click on **Product variation types**.

4. The default Drupal Commerce install creates a single product variation definition for us, but we are going to delete this one, so we can go through the exercise of setting one up from scratch.

5. Delete the **Product** type as shown in the following screenshot:

6. Click on **Add product variation** type and make a new one called Foodstuff, as shown in the following screenshot:

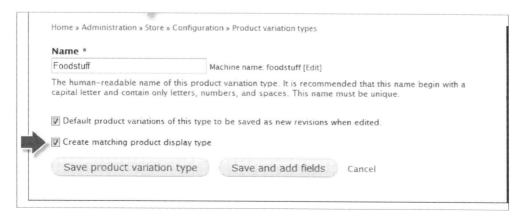

7. Make sure that you leave **Create matching product display type** ticked, then click on **Save and add fields** and you will be taken to the **manage fields** page, that is **Defining product fields**.

Our initial product definition has fields for the product's SKU, Title, Price, and Status.

We need to add new fields to represent the image, pack size, and the physical weight of our products.

Adding an Image field

The following are the steps to add an `Image` field:

1. Create a field called `Product image` of type **Image** as shown in the following screenshot:

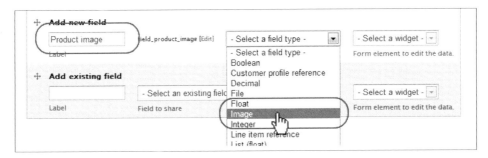

2. In the **FIELD SETTINGS** page, you can accept the defaults and click on **Save field settings**.

You will then be taken, as per normal Drupal field handling, to the field's edit page.

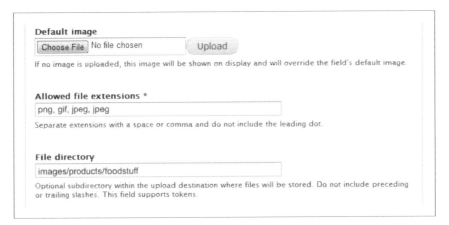

A handy tip here is to upload a **No file chosen** image as the default image for your products. This will then be used until you have added an image to your products.

The field's edit page has quite a few other settings, detailed in the following table:

Field	Suggested value and notes
Label	Product image
Required field	No (in case you don't have an image available)
Help text	Add some help text for your store owner or administrators here.
Default image	Leave blank or upload a **No file chosen** placeholder.
Allowed field extensions	Accept the defaults of png, gif, jpg, jpeg
File directory	Images/products/foodstuff (so that like product images are filed neatly together should we later wish to browse them or even export them. This folder structure is relative to <drupal installation>/sites/default/files path.
Maximum image resolution	Leave blank
Minimum image resolution	Leave blank
Maximum upload size	1 MB
Enable Alt field	Yes
Enable Title field	No
Preview image style	Thumbnail
Progress indicator	Accept the default

Adding a Pack size (Taxonomy) field

For the pack size, we will add another field of type **Term reference**, which will be a reference to a term from the Pack size taxonomy vocabulary.

For the purposes of this example, we will assume that there are a number of standard pack sizes that apply to all of the products.

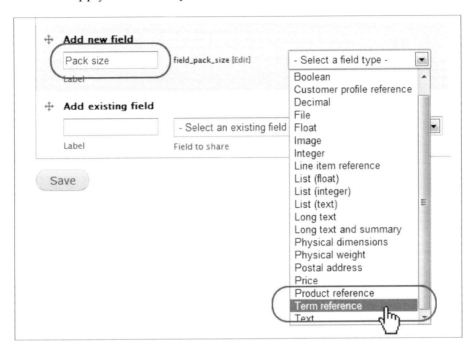

Complete the final page of settings as follows:

Field	Suggested value and notes
Label	`Pack size`
Required field	Yes. This will ensure that every product variation has a unique title, and thus aid the shoppers in choosing the particular one they are after.
Help text	Include a note to say that whatever is chosen here will form part of the unique product variation title.

Pack size as variation picker

Finally, you may notice that Commerce has added in another section entitled **ATTRIBUTE FIELD SETTINGS**.

We want our **Pack size** field to function in such a way as to provide the shopper with a choice drop-down menu that enables them to pick the precise sellable product variation that they wish to buy when it comes to the point of **Add to cart**.

Ticking **Enable this field to function as an attribute field on Add to Cart forms**, as shown in the following screenshot, will do just that:

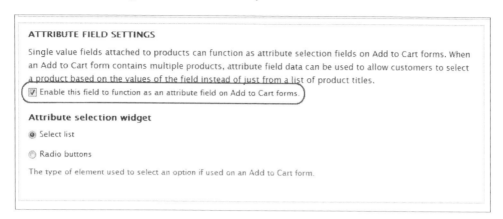

Adding a physical weight field

Adding an actual physical weight for our products is the first configuration step outside of Drupal Commerce core functionality. We could add this value using one of the default field types, such as text or number, but if we use physical weights now, it will help us later when we are working on shipping.

We will need to download and install the following additional modules:

- http://drupal.org/project/physical
- http://drupal.org/project/commerce_physical

Once you have done this, go back to the field product field's page again and you will see a new option in the drop-down menu for field types, as shown in the following screenshot:

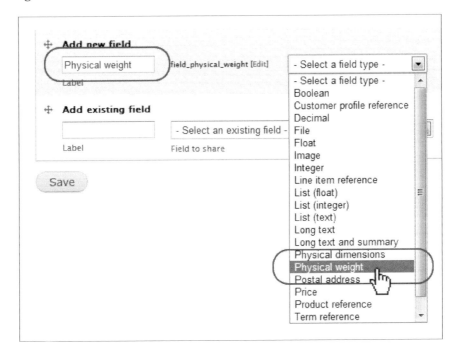

There is nothing configurable in the second screen for this field type so you can move straight onto the **Settings** page.

In the settings for this field, you can set the unit of measurement. For our purposes, I have selected **Grams**.

Defining the product (display) node

The **Foodstuff** product display node that was automatically created and associated with the product variation type we just created, can now be modified to meet the needs of our site.

> Once again, I find it useful to think of the product as the customer facing description of one or more products. For example, if a product is available in three sizes, and therefore has three products in the store, the description is more than likely identical for each.

Given that the **Foodstuff** product node is the browsable shop front it makes good sense that a field is added here to contain the product description rather than in the product variation.

Since the **Foodstuff** product node type is a conventional node type, we can access it via the normal route.

From the toolbar, navigate to **Structure | Content types**. You will notice that in addition to the two default content types defined in the Drupal install, we now have a new one named **Foodstuff**.

Click on **manage fields**, as shown in the following screenshot, and we will define some additional information about our products.

As well as the default **Title** field, there is a **Product variations** field of type **Product reference**.

This field is the key to enable you to associate the product display node with one or more product variations.

To supplement these, add a description field of type **Long Text** with the **Text Area** widget. Click on **Save and accept all the default values**.

Variation management

Finally, to improve the shop owner's product management experience further, enable the Inline Entity Form module that you downloaded earlier. This new additional module provides a new widget for use with the **Product reference** type field, that is, our **Product variations** field.

Revisiting the **Manage fields** page should reveal that the module has automatically applied the new widget for the Foodstuff content type for the product variation field.

Catalog structure

We now have our basic product definition ready. Next, we must define some structure for the catalog so that customers can find our products easily.

From the toolbar, navigate to **Structure | Taxonomy**. Considering our products, we want the customer to be able to browse the website like a catalog, so it makes sense to create a catalog taxonomy with broad sections for each of the types of product we offer.

We may also want to show the customer all of the products by their favorite brand, so we will add a **Brand** taxonomy to start with as well. Click on **Add vocabulary**. Create a vocabulary for **Catalog** and another for **Brand**.

Having set up these two vocabularies, the next step is to attach them to the product display node, the Foodstuff content type, so that once we have created one or more actual instances of product display nodes, we can classify them.

Next, go back to the **Manage fields** page of the **Foodstuff** product display. Navigate to **Structure | Content Types | Foodstuff | manage fields**.

Add a new **Term reference** type field, called **Catalog** using the **Select Checkbox/ radio buttons widget**. On the **FIELD SETTINGS** page, select the **Catalog** vocabulary as shown in the following screenshot:

Next, repeat the process to add the **Brand** taxonomy reference field.

After a bit of field order rearrangement, your product display field's page should now look like the following screenshot:

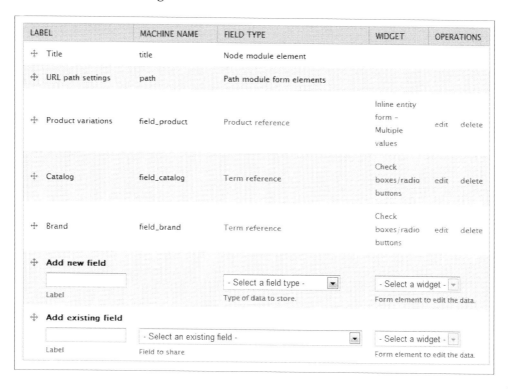

Note that I have left the **Term reference** fields' widget set to the (default) **Check boxes / radio buttons**. This is adequate for our small demonstration catalog, but we could of course adjust it to a select list if our catalog was to grow significantly.

Entering product data

All of our product structures are ready to go, so we can set up some products.

If you have lots of products in your store, you may want to look into the mass import option. This is beyond the scope of this book, but start by looking into the Feeds module on `Drupal.org`.

Adding taxonomy terms

Before we start adding products, we need to go into the taxonomy and create the catalog sections and brands we set up earlier.

In our coffee wholesale scenario, we have the following terms with which we want to be able to classify our Products:

- Fairtrade Coffee
    ◦ Coffee Options
    ◦ Coffee Beans
    ◦ Ground Coffee
    ◦ Instant Coffee

- Disposables
- Equipment
- Fairtrade and Organic Teas
- Gifts
- Other Fair trade Products
- Sundries

Note that there is a hierarchy in the Fairtrade section. The following are the steps to add taxonomy terms:

1. From the toolbar, navigate to **Structure | Taxonomy**.
2. Then click on **add terms** next to the **Catalog** vocabulary.
3. You can then add the appropriate sections (terms) for your store.
4. Add each term simply by typing out to the word(s) and hitting the *Enter* key; after each term is saved you will remain on the same page so that you can click and type the next one.

Don't concern yourself about the hierarchy of terms; we'll adjust the relative positions of each term later, for now just get them all entered.

NAME	OPERATIONS
✛ Coffee Beans	edit
✛ Coffee Options	edit
✛ Disposables	edit
✛ Equipment	edit
✛ Fairtrade and Organic Teas	edit
✛ Fairtrade Coffee	edit
✛ Gifts	edit
✛ Ground Coffee	edit
✛ Instant Coffee	edit
✛ Other Fairtrade Products	edit
✛ Sundries	edit

Note that, after entering the term, the Drupal Taxonomy module has positioned the term alphabetically amongst all of the other pre-existing ones. This will not necessarily be correct for all sites and certainly doesn't in ours, given that we have the hierarchical Fairtrade section, so we now go and re-order and re-position the terms by dragging them around by their drag handles until we have precisely what we are after.

Similarly, add some dummy brand names to the **Brands** vocabulary.

Adding products

Given that we are using the Inline Entity Form module, we can create actual sellable products from directly inside a Product display node. I'll take you step-by-step through the process now.

From the toolbar, navigate to **Content | Add Content**. You will see a list of all of the currently defined content types.

Our **Foodstuff** product display node type isn't showing there. That's because Commerce noted that it was the one created automatically when we created our **Foodstuff** product variation, so it (Commerce) hides it away in a special tab entitled **ADD PRODUCT**. Click on the **ADD PRODUCT** tab as shown in the following screenshot:

Select **Foodstuff**. Now, here's the clever bit provided for us by the Inline Entity Form module; we are actually able to add or edit any number of sellable products from directly within the **Foodstuff** node that we are using to group them.

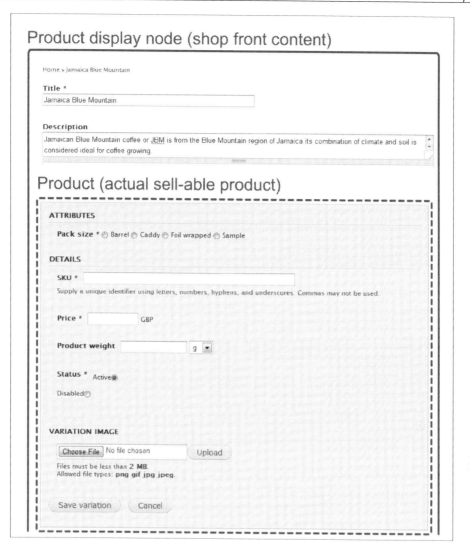

The create product screen is quite long, so we can look at the two sections highlighted in the preceding screenshot.

Product (display)

The first product we are going to create is `Jamaica Blue Mountain Coffee`, which is available in four pack sizes.

So, we set the overall **Title** field to Jamaica Blue Mountain and we can add in the **Description** field of the product as a whole, as shown in the following screenshot:

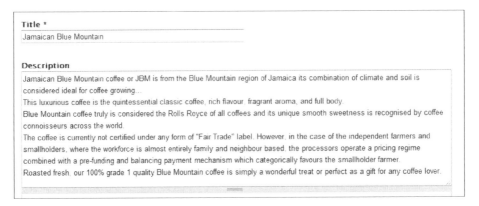

Product variations

We now set the variation for the first pack size with its unique data combination of **Pack size**, **SKU**, **Price**, **Product weight**, **Image**, and accompanying **Alternate text** as shown in the following screenshot:

Click on **Save variation** to commit the new product to the database and you will save the first variation in-line on the product (display) node edit form.

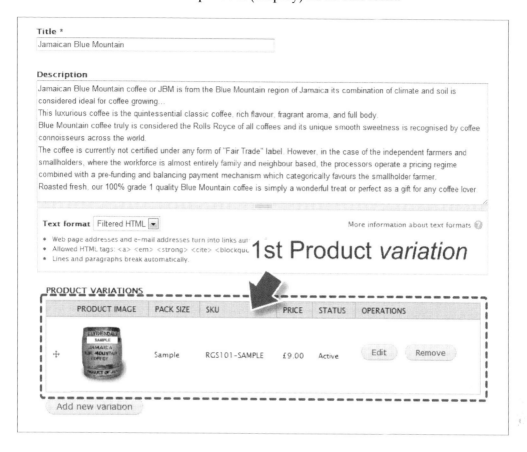

Once all of the variations have been created, the screen looks like the following screenshot:

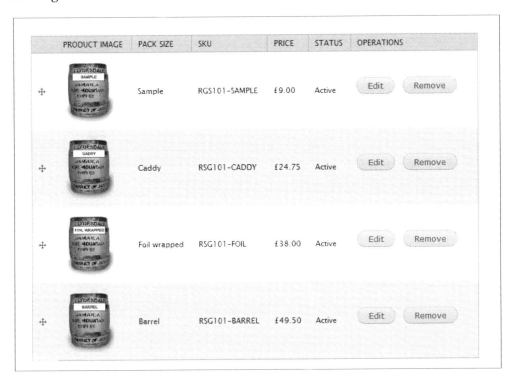

	PRODUCT IMAGE	PACK SIZE	SKU	PRICE	STATUS	OPERATIONS
✛		Sample	RGS101-SAMPLE	£9.00	Active	Edit Remove
✛		Caddy	RSG101-CADDY	£24.75	Active	Edit Remove
✛		Foil wrapped	RSG101-FOIL	£38.00	Active	Edit Remove
✛		Barrel	RSG101-BARREL	£49.50	Active	Edit Remove

At the bottom of the screen are the so-called vertical tabs which contain more detailed information about the Product (display) as a whole.

Product catalog

The **Product catalog** tab contains all of the taxonomy reference fields you defined for this product variation type.

So here you can select a **Catalog** and **Brand** classification for the product as shown in the following screenshot:

Menu settings

Menu settings defines whether there is an entry for the product page in any of the site navigation menus. Unless you have a small number of products, it's unlikely that you would have a menu linking directly to a product.

URL path settings

The URL path indicates what the browser's web address will be to get to this product page.

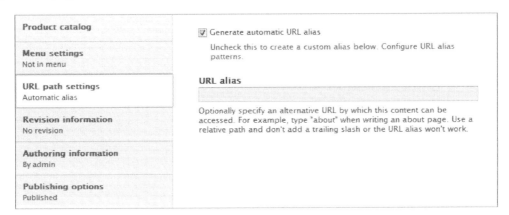

Since we are using the Pathauto module, our URL alias for our product will match the title once we save. If you wish to set the URL alias directly, simply un-tick the **Generate automatic URL alias** check and add your own manually.

You can also optionally set up patterns of URL based on the fields in the product. Moreover, you can set up specific URL alias patterns for each product type if you wish so that, for example, all coffee products have the ../products/coffee/<product title> URL.

Revision information

Revision information allows you to specify whether a new revision is saved if you make changes. Also you can add a revision log to record the reasons for the change.

Authoring information

Authoring information shows who was editing the product last and when, as shown in the following screenshot:

Publishing options

Publishing options shows whether the product is live on the website and if it has been promoted, as shown in the following screenshot:

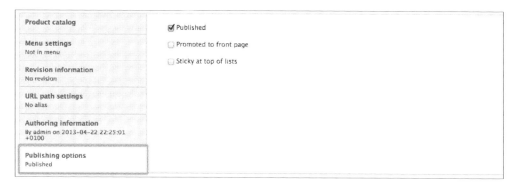

Displaying the product

Now that you have finished defining your first product, click on the **View** tab to see what it looks like on your website, as shown in the following screenshot:

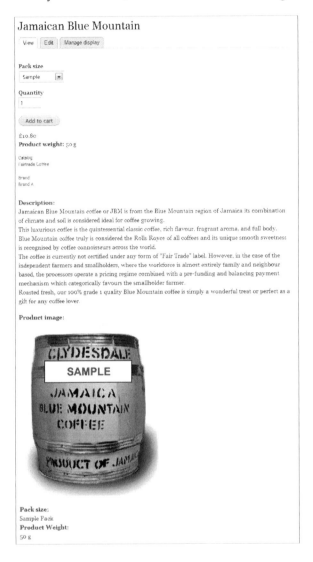

As you can see, everything is there, but the layout leaves something to be desired.

Notice that if you change the **Product variation** drop-down menu, the **Price**, **Product image**, and **Pack size** values will also change. Thus, this drop-down menu is allowing the customer to view the difference between the product variations before selecting which one to add to their cart.

Refining the layout

To help us modify the layout easily, we are going to install a new module, Display suite, available at `http://drupal.org/project/ds`.

Enable the Display suite and Display suite UI modules and then go back to the product's view page.

You should now see a new tab at the top of the product, **Manage display** as shown in the following screenshot:

You can control the layout for any particular view of the product; by default the teaser (or list) view and default view are different, but you can also add other variations for the search result, for example.

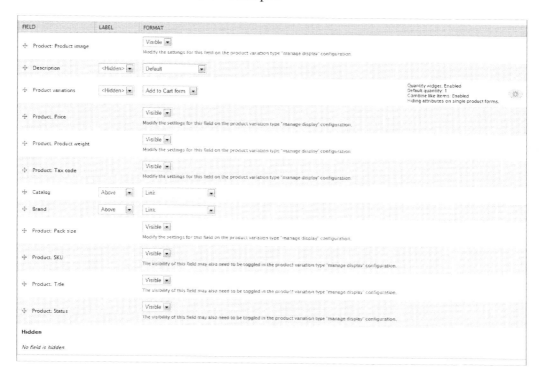

On this screen, you can change the order of the fields shown and change the visibility of their field labels.

If you click the **Layout for foodstuff in default** vertical tab, you will see a list of predefined grids that you can use to easily lay out the products; for example, selecting the **Two column** option as shown in the following screenshot:

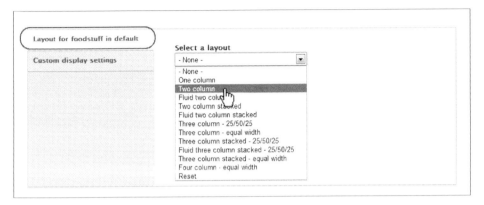

You must click on the **Save** button to confirm the choice and when the page reloads, you will see that you can now arrange the fields into **Left** and **Right** regions.

Disable the unwanted fields and arrange **Left** or **Right** as shown in the following screenshot:

Some fields (marked with a red asterisk above) are actually referencing the product variations themselves, so you can click through to the equivalent **manage display** for these to control the details of these fields' layout, as shown in the following screenshot:

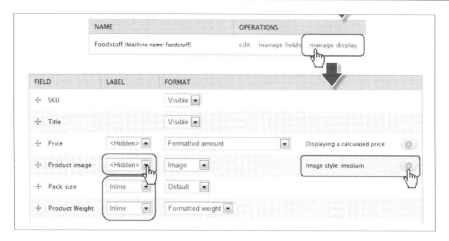

After removing any unnecessary labels, reducing the image display to a smaller style, and changing the order of the fields, the view of your product should look like the following screenshot:

Adding to cart field behavior

The **Add to Cart** field controls the association between the product display and the product variations. You can make some changes to the settings to modify the view of the page.

Navigate to **manage display** and then click on the cog on the product variations field, as shown in the following screenshot:

The options will expand, as in the following screenshot:

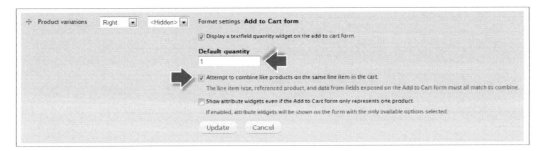

The options are as follows:

- **Display a textfield quantity widget on the add to cart form**: If you uncheck this box, the quantity field is not shown on the **Add to Cart** button. The customer can still change the quantity of their order at the cart stage.

- **Default quantity**: The number of the product added to the cart initially, even if the quantity widget is hidden.

- **Attempt to combine like products on the same line item in the cart**: If checked, the quantity in the cart will be incremented if the customer attempts to add the same product more than once.

 Most of the time you would want the line items to combine when the customer clicks on **Add to Cart** more than once; however this option exists for scenarios such as personalized products, where you might buy more than one item, but they would be distinctly different line items.

- **Show attribute widgets even if the Add to Cart form only represents one product**: By default, this is unchecked which means that if a product display only references one product variation (for example, the product only comes in one size), there is no drop-down shown for the customer to select a product variation.

Summary

At the end of this chapter, you now have a complete product catalog with some sample data in place. We have covered the concepts of defining products, product displays, and how you can add custom fields to your products.

It's been a long chapter, but now you are ready to add some e-commerce functionality.

5
Shopping Cart

Now that we have products defined and a catalog structure, we need to provide a way for customers to collect items together in a shopping cart in order to make a purchase.

You may have noticed that we already have an **Add to Cart** button on the **Product** display that enables the customer to add a specified **Quantity** of a product.

In Drupal Commerce, there are a number of ways to display the cart, and as ever, they are all controlled by Views which makes it very easy to customize them.

The Shopping cart page

When a customer clicks on the **Add to Cart** button on a product, the default behavior for Commerce is to simply display a message telling the user that the item has been added to their cart, and clicking on the link will take them straight to the cart as shown in the following screenshot:

This basic view shows **Product**, **Price**, **Quantity**, and **Total** as well as giving the customer basic controls to remove products and update quantities.

Hover over the top- right-hand corner of the table next to **Total** and click on the gear icon. You will see an **Edit view** link.

This master view of the shopping cart looks like the following screenshot:

The **Views** interface can be quite daunting at first, so let's visit each section in turn.

Format

The shopping cart is displayed as a table. This is a sensible default as we are showing multiple values for each order line and a summary at the bottom. However, you can change the format for theming purposes.

Fields

The view shows a list of Line Items associated with an Order. In Drupal Commerce, a cart and an order are the same thing—just set at a different status.

The fields we expect to see here are present: **Title**, **Unit price**, **Quantity**, a **Delete** button, and **Total**.

You may also have noticed the **Display** path— this is not visible in our cart table, but it's used as an excluded field to provide a link back to the product display that was used to add this item to the cart.

Filter criteria

The filters make sure that we are only displaying line items of a **Product type**, that is, any additional types of line items that have been defined are excluded from the cart. These may include things such as shipping or discount lines.

Sort criteria

The default sort order is to show items by **Line item ID**—this is a sensible choice as it will then reflect the order in which the customer added the items to their cart.

Footer

The footer has a special summary field—**Line item summary**. If you edit this field, you will see a few more settings that are available as shown in the following screenshot:

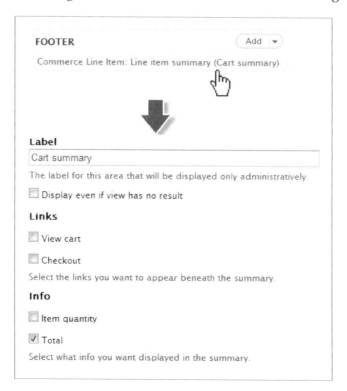

Advanced

One essential inclusion is in **Advanced | Contextual Filters**.

You will see a value for **Order ID**. This ensures that the cart displayed contains only the line items for the current user's order.

Customizing the Cart page

You can add additional fields from the Commerce line item entity. If you are using custom line item types (for example, for personalized products), any field you have added will be available to add to the view.

You can also change the order of the cart view columns using the **Rearrange** button.

The Cart block

It is common to have a shopping cart summary block in the side bar or header of a website.

Drupal Commerce provides a cart block which is disabled by default. To enable this block:

1. From the toolbar, go to **Structure | Blocks**.
2. Move the shopping cart block into the **Sidebar second** region.
3. Go back to your home page, and you will now see a new mini shopping cart view as shown in the following screenshot:

This view is very similar to the cart page and you can edit the view in the same way if you want to modify it.

Summary

In this chapter we explored the shopping cart and shopping cart blocks. In addition to browsing the catalogue, our customer can now select the things that they would like to buy by adding them to a cart. The next step is to build the checkout process.

6
Checkout

Before starting this chapter, ensure that, in addition to the existing Customer module, you also have the Customer UI module enabled.

The checkout in Drupal Commerce is highly configurable.

You can have a multistep checkout process or combine all of the steps into a single page depending on your design. There are two important definitions to understand: **checkout pane** and **checkout page**.

Checkout pages

From the toolbar, navigate to **Store** | **Configuration** | **Checkout settings**.

There are three checkout pages initially defined. They are as follows:

- **Checkout**: This is the main checkout page, which allows the customer to add their account and billing information. When we add more features to our store later on, more checkout panes will appear in the checkout page.

- **Review order**: The final page before the payment is taken is referred to as the review order page. It gives the customer a final chance to see all of the order in one place before committing to buy. This is a legal requirement in some territories.

- **Checkout complete**: This is a confirmation page displayed at the end of the order process informing the customer of their order number and displaying a thank you message.

Checkout panes

Within each Checkout page there are a number of Checkout panes. You can rearrange the order of these here to determine the order they render in your checkout process.

Each checkout pane has its own configuration page.

Pane settings

All panes have a common display settings area allowing you to decide if the pane is collapsible and whether it will appear on the order review page.

Each pane can be configured separately via the configure link on the right-hand side. As an example, let's look at the settings for the **Shopping cart** contents pane. You can opt to have each pane appear visually different.

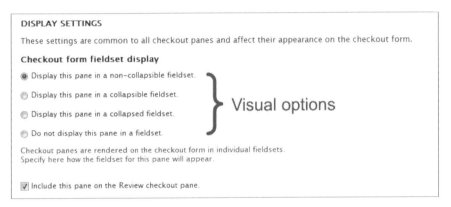

Underneath this are the settings specific to the checkout pane.

For the **Shopping cart** contents pane, the only option is to change the view used to display the cart.

If you choose to use a different view from the default one, then you can still modify it in the same manner discussed in *Chapter 5, Shopping Cart*.

Account information

The account information pane allows you to specify double entry of e-mail for anonymous users. This prevents typos and ensures that you have a valid contact for the customer.

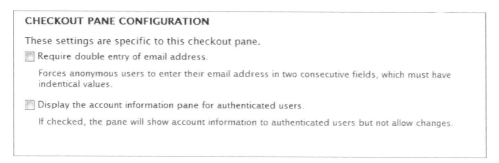

If the customer is already logged into the website, you don't need them to enter their e-mail address, so the second option allows you to select whether or not you would like to show the customer their details anyway at this stage.

Billing information

The billing information pane is used to collect the customer's address details. If there are multiple customer profile types, we can specify which one is used in the checkout pane, as shown in the following screenshot:

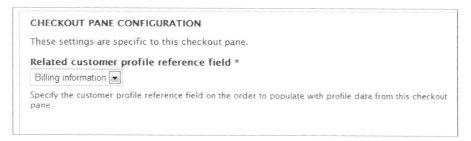

Completion message

By default, a simple thank you message is displayed at the end of the checkout process.

You can modify this in the settings for the completion message pane, as shown in the following screenshot:

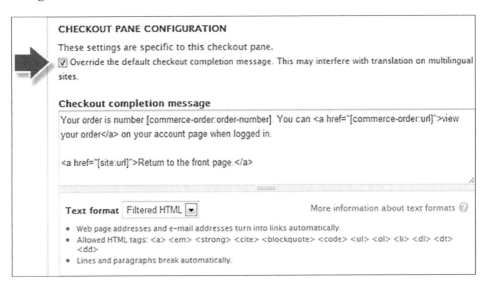

Checkout rules

One of the major dependencies of Drupal Commerce is the Rules module.

Rules is a powerful and highly configurable system of events, conditions, and actions which make the progress of the order possible.

There are a number of default checkout rules defined, which we can use to illustrate how Rules work, using the following steps:

1. From the toolbar, navigate to **Store | Configuration | Checkout settings**.
2. Then click onto the **CHECKOUT RULES** tab, as shown in the following screenshot:

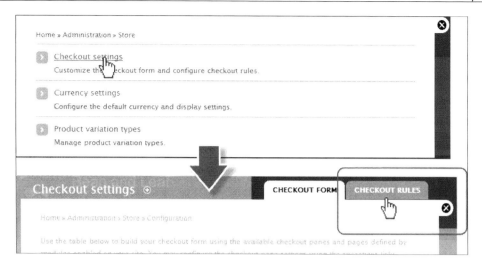

How a rule works

Click on **edit** on the first rules.

A rule consists of one or more **Events**, which will start the rule when they occur. In this case, the event is **Completing the checkout process**. Drupal Commerce will trigger this event when the customer completes the last pane in the checkout process.

Next, the rules will evaluate the **Conditions** to determine if the rule should continue. These conditions are extensive, but in this case, we want this rule to run every time.

Finally, the rules will fire one or more Actions in response to the rule event. The actions available are dependent on the event and conditions. In this case, we want to change the order state to pending, which means that the order will move from being a cart to being an order.

Other default rules

The default installation has a number of other preset rules that you should also understand.

Assigning an anonymous order to a pre-existing user

If we allow anonymous customers to place orders, that is, we do not require them to register an account on the Drupal site, we are still collecting their e-mail address as part of the order process.

If the e-mail address used matches an existing account on the website, this rule will assign the order to that account for the customer's convenience.

If you do not want this behavior, you can disable this rule.

Creating a new account for an anonymous order

This rule also applies in the scenario where the customer does not have an account on the Drupal site. When the order completes, a new account is set up and the customer is notified of this by e-mail.

Again, you may not require this behavior, so the rule can be disabled.

Sending an order notification e-mail

The customer is e-mailed a receipt with their order number when the order process completes. This is standard behavior for an e-commerce site, but you may want to modify the rule to change the text of the e-mail sent.

Payment gateways

It is possible to set up a Commerce site without a payment step, but it is quite unusual. We will now enable some more modules to allow you to collect payment from your customers.

Enable the following modules from the Commerce package:

- Order UI
- Payment
- Payment Method Example
- Payment UI

Now, go back to the checkout settings page by navigating to **Store | Configuration | Checkout settings**.

There will be a new checkout pane in the review checkout page.

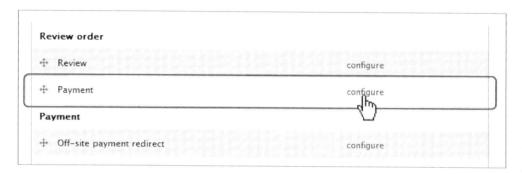

The payment checkout pane has one setting that allows you to prevent checkout, if no payment gateway is available, as shown in the following screenshot:

You can use this functionality to quickly disable the ordering process of your store without taking the whole site offline.

Selecting a payment gateway

The choice of payment gateway is usually dictated by the business requirements rather than the technology. Before signing up with a payment provider, it is worth checking that there is a payment gateway module available for Drupal Commerce.

A quick reference for this is `http://drupalcommerce.org/`.

It is possible to set up multiple payment methods so that the customer has a choice when they reach the end of the checkout process.

For demonstration purposes, we will use the simple PayPal gateway available at `http://drupal.org/project/commerce_paypal`.

Types of payment gateway integration

There are generally three types of payment gateway integrations that you can use. Each has advantages and disadvantages, and also slightly different legal and compliance requirements.

Offsite redirection

At the end of the checkout process, the customer is taken to the payment provider's website to enter their card details.

When the payment has been completed, the customer is returned to the checkout complete page on your website. The following are the advantages and disadvantages of offsite redirection:

Advantages	Disadvantages
You do not have to worry about security certificates or credit card numbers. Customers may be more comfortable while entering their credit card details when they recognize the payment provider (especially if you are a small store).	The checkout process is limited, as you always need to go offsite to complete the process.

Inline

An inline frame (or iframe) element is created in the payment checkout pane. This displays as page from the payment provider site within your checkout, and therefore, appears to be integrated. The following are the advantages and disadvantages of the iframe element:

Advantages	Disadvantages
• Card entry is still at the payment provider so they hold the risk. • You have more control over the design of the checkout.	• The iframe will be a payment provider controlled page, so you may not have control of how it looks.

Direct

Drupal Commerce provides a credit card data form in the payment checkout pane. The communication with the payment provider gateway happens in the background and the customer never leaves the website.

Advantages	Disadvantages
• You have full control of the checkout process. • You can include payment at any step. • Direct integration allows you to perform more actions, such as refunds and voids of orders.	• The legal responsibility for protection of card data is with you rather than the payment provider.

Setting up PayPal

The following are the steps for setting up PayPal:

1. Enable the following modules from the Commerce (PayPal) package:
   - PayPal
   - PayPal WPS

2. From the toolbar, navigate to **Store | Configuration | Payment methods**, as shown in the following screenshot:

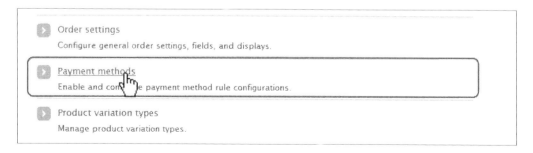

3. You will see the example payment method that we installed earlier and the PayPal **Web Payments Standard (WPS)** payment method set as disabled, as shown in the following screenshot:

4. Now click on **Enable payment method: PayPal WPS**, so that it is the only enabled gateway.

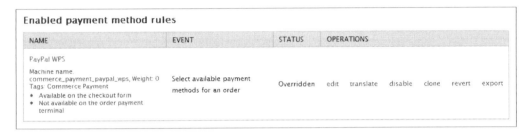

5. The WPS gateway is controlled by a Rule, similar to almost everything else in Commerce, and settings for PayPal integration can be found by clicking on **edit** on the payment method rule, and then **edit** again, next to the Rule's payment action, as shown in the following screenshot:

6. Each payment gateway will provide different settings depending on the options available.

7. You need to have a PayPal account associated with an e-mail address.

8. Select your currency, language preference, and so on.

9. Then click on **Save**.

This is all you need to do to active PayPal as a payment option.

The customers' view

If we now return to the frontend of the website, we can review what the customer will see during the checkout process.

Before we do this, we need to set some permission for the checkout, using the following steps:

1. From the toolbar, click on **People** and then click on the **PERMISSIONS** tab, as shown in the following screenshot:

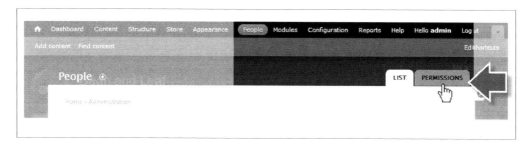

2. The default installation of Drupal Commerce does not enable the checkout for any role, except administrator. In most circumstances, you will want anonymous customers to be able to checkout. Set the following permissions for **ANONYMOUS USER** and **AUTHENTICATED USER**: Checkout | Access checkout

Customer view of the Checkout page

The **Checkout** page looks like the following screenshot:

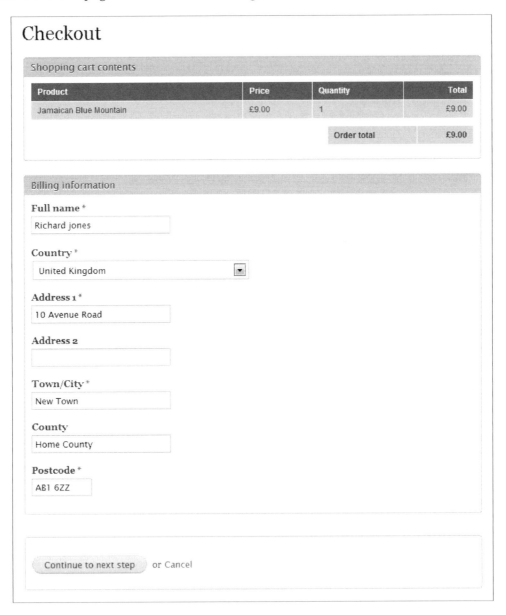

Customer view of the Review order and Payment page

The **Review Order** and **Payment** page looks like the following screenshot:

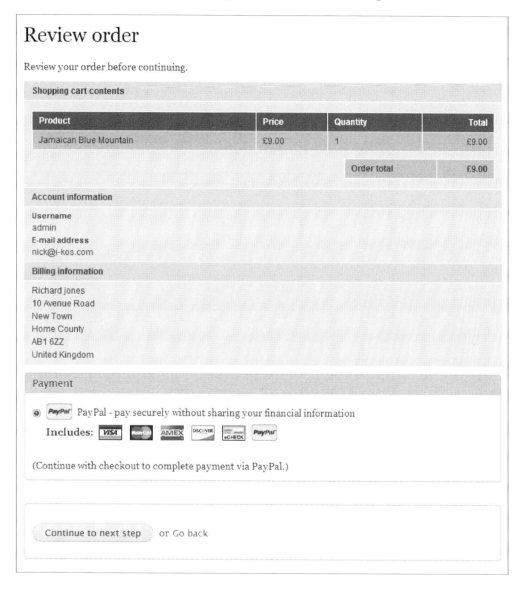

Finally, after continuing you will momentarily see a message telling you that you are about to be redirected to PayPal.

Customer view of Order complete

After payment, you will then be taken back to a confirmation page on your shop site.

Summary

Congratulations! At the end of this chapter you have a working Drupal Commerce installation that is able to accept payments from the public. You have set up and customized the checkout process and connected Drupal Commerce to PayPal.

The next chapters will show you how to enhance the e-commerce experience for the customer and the store owner.

7
Shipping

If you are selling physical goods, you need to get them to the customer. Shipping can be a complex area as the cost of shipping can vary greatly depending on the type of goods and destination. Often, you will also want to give customers a choice of shipping, for example, a premium next day service.

To get started, download the following modules:

- http://www.drupal.org/project/commerce_shipping
- http://www.drupal.org/project/commerce_flat_rate

Go to the modules page and enable:

- Commerce Shipping
- Commerce Shipping UI
- Commerce Flat Rate

You will now have a new page available in the store configuration. From the Toolbar, navigate to:

Store | Configuration | Shipping

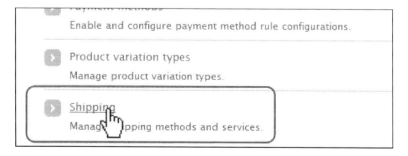

Definition of terms

The following terms are important to understand when setting up shipping. Commerce is using industry standards, but the difference between a shipping method and shipping service can be subtle:

- Shipping method
- Shipping service

Shipping method

A shipping method is the physical method of moving the order—for example UPS, FedEx, and Royal Mail.

In this chapter we will be looking at the **Flat Rate** shipping method which allows you to calculate the shipping for an order, but does not integrate with any third-party systems.

Shipping service

A shipping service is what will be presented to the customer—for example, Standard delivery, Express delivery, and so on.

Setting up our Flat Rate shipping services

For our store, we will be setting up the following shipping rules:

- Standard delivery (3-5 days): £4.50
- Express delivery (next day): £9.00

Click on **Add a flat rate service**, as shown in the following screenshot:

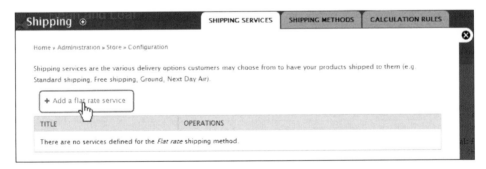

Next, add the first of your options—Standard delivery at a rate of £4.50 as shown in the following screenshot:

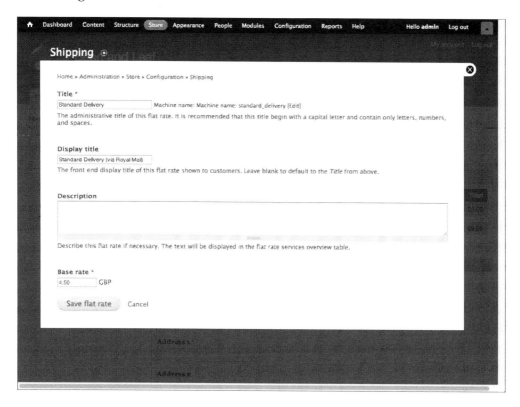

Then the second option can be added as follows:

Title	Express delivery
Display Title	Express delivery (via Royal Mail)
Description	Express delivery (next day): £9.00
Base Rate	9.00

When you have set both of these up, the screen should look like the following screenshot:

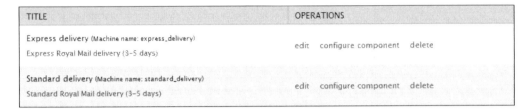

TITLE	OPERATIONS
Express delivery (Machine name: express_delivery) Express Royal Mail delivery (3-5 days)	edit configure component delete
Standard delivery (Machine name: standard_delivery) Standard Royal Mail delivery (3-5 days)	edit configure component delete

The output shown to the customer

Now that we have set up the checkout panes, we need to consider how this will look from the customer's perspective.

Shipping address

The Shipping module adds an extra customer profile type; a shipping profile which is used to collect the customer's delivery address during checkout.

Thus, when proceeding on from the Cart, your customers will be asked for their Shipping address and Billing address as shown in the following screenshot:

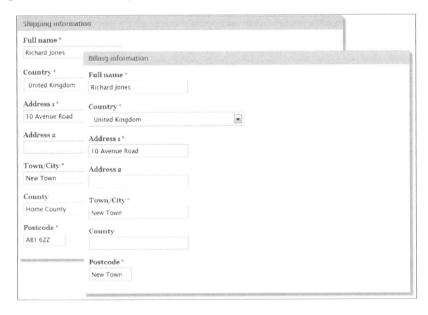

In the Checkout Pane Configuration settings for this address (the shipping service pane on the checkout settings page), there are now additional options available as shown in the following screenshot:

Require a shipping service at all times, preventing checkout if none are available: If this is ticked, the checkout process will stop if there are no shipping services available that match the conditions of the order.

 If you limit the shipping of your orders to a specific set of countries, you can limit the shipping rules to the countries you ship to and enable the **Require a shipping service at all times** option. This will prevent an order being placed for delivery to a country that you do not export to.

There is now an extra page in the checkout process, which presents the customer with their shipping options as shown in the following screenshot:

Calculating shipping rates via AJAX

Shipping rates are often calculated based on geographical destination. However, if we move the shipping checkout pane onto the same checkout page that we are using to collect the delivery address, we are unable to calculate the appropriate shipping services without refreshing the page. This option uses AJAX to load the shipping services available as soon as the address details are updated.

Presenting different shipping services based on the order conditions

So far we have presented the customer with a Standard or Express shipping option. However, we may charge different amounts if the customer wants to ship the order internationally, or if they place a large order.

We can set up multiple shipping services, and then set conditions to determine whether they are presented to the customer.

Free shipping when you spend a certain amount

A common scenario is to set up a free shipping option when the customer spends above a certain threshold.

Go to the **Shipping services** page again and click on **Add a flat rate service**. Fill in the details and a ZERO base rate, then click on **Save**.

You will now see your new shipping service alongside the two that we created earlier.

Click on **configure component** next to the free delivery service.

International shipping exempt from free shipping

To develop our scenario further, we do not want to offer the free shipping option to customers outside of the UK, so we must include a check to see that the qualifying order is actually being shipped within the UK.

Go back to the free shipping service and click on **configure component** again as shown in the following screenshot:

Add another condition; the **Order address component comparison** as shown in the following screenshot:

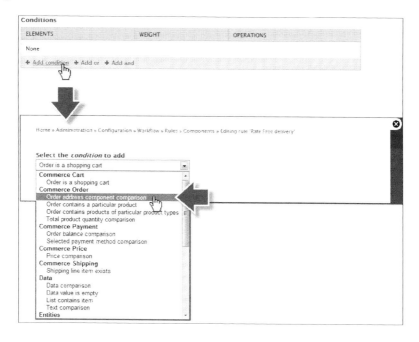

Select the value for the **Address** field as **Address**, and for the **ADDRESS COMPONENT** field select **Country** from the dropdown as shown in the following screenshot:

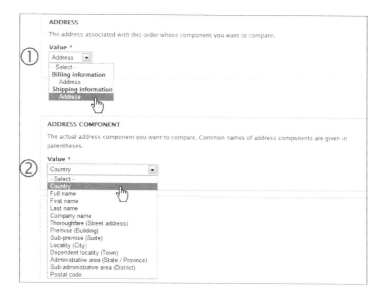

Then enter the ISO value of the country, in this case GB, as shown in the following screenshot:

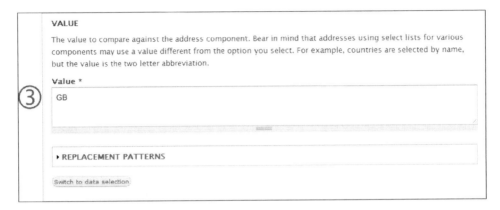

Essentially then, the condition that we just added checks whether the shipping country is GB.

You should see your finished condition in place as shown in the following screenshot:

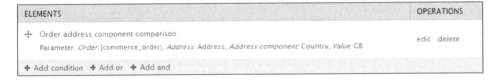

Go back to the checkout page and experiment with changing the shipping country—you should see the free delivery shipping service disappear if you select any shipping country other than the United Kingdom.

Checking the value of the order value is above a certain threshold

We want to check whether the order balance is more than £50 in order for it to qualify for free shipping, so we need to add another Condition.

Select **Order balance comparison** from the dropdown menu, as shown in the following screenshot:

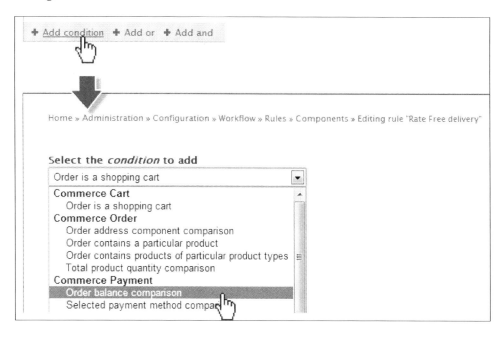

Select the >= operator and enter 5000 as the value.

Now, go back to the cart and change the quantity of items in the cart to increase the order value.

When you check out you will see the additional free shipping option is now available as shown in the following screenshot:

In this scenario you would probably want to add the inverse condition to the original Standard delivery service (that is, check whether the order balance is less than **5000**), so that the customer is only presented with the free delivery option and express shipping.

Different billing and shipping addresses

Now that you have enabled the shipping modules, you will see two customer profiles during the checkout to collect the billing and shipping addresses, respectively. Often, these addresses will be the same and customers find it very frustrating to have to enter the same details twice. To improve your checkout process, go back to the checkout settings page and perform the following set of instructions:

1. Navigate to **Store | Configuration | Checkout Settings**.

2. Click on configure next to the **Billing information** pane in the **Checkout** group.

3. Tick the **Enable profile copying on this checkout pane** checkbox leaving the rest of the default values set, as shown in the following screenshot:

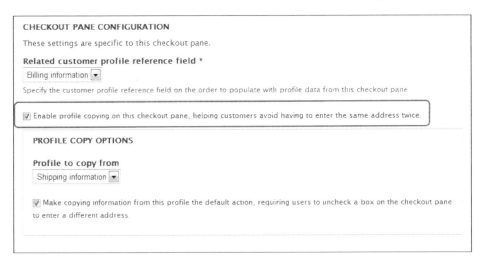

4. Now, when the customer goes to the checkout they will see as screen as shown in the following screenshot:

If they deselect the checkbox, they can fill in an alternative address. You can also do this the other way round, so that the customer fills in the billing address, and the shipping address is assumed.

Order tracking

Customers expect to know when their order will arrive. You can use the order status codes in Drupal Commerce to indicate the progress of the order.

When the order is initially placed, the order status will be set to **Pending**. You can then use the **Complete** status to indicate when you have shipped the order.

Additionally, you can define a new field in the Order type definition, named tracking code, which can be presented to the user when they view their order history.

1. Go to: **Store | Configuration | Order Settings | Manage Fields**
2. **Add a new text field called** Tracking Code**.**
3. Now edit the view **User Orders** and add the new field. Now when a customer views their order history list, they can see the tracking number as well.

Advanced order tracking

This method of tracking orders is quite labor intensive for the site owner—it requires the status to be updated when the order moves through the shipping process. However, there are other modules available that integrate directly with popular courier services, such as UPS and USPS. An up to date list is available on the Commerce Shipping module page: `http://drupal.org/project/commerce_shipping`.

Summary

At the end of this chapter you have the basic information that you need to set up complex shipping rules and conditions for your orders based on a Flat Rate system. It is also possible to create shipping rules based on the weight or value of the order.

8
Tax

Depending on the type of store, trading location, and volume of sales, you may need to set up sales tax or Value Added Tax rules for your store.

Value added Tax (VAT) is standard in most of the European Union.

The price displayed to the customer must be the final selling price including the VAT.

In other parts of the world, including the USA, sales tax is added at the checkout. This means that prices are displayed throughout the site without tax, and the tax amount is calculated and added to the total during the checkout process.

Drupal Commerce handles both of these scenarios by declaring two tax types, which handle each type of scenario.

Tax types and tax rates

Like tax types, you can have different tax rates as well. Tax rates may vary based on the location of the store, as is the case in the United States, where tax rates vary per state. In the EU, VAT rates may vary based on the type of products being sold. For example, in the UK, most products are taxed at 20 percent, except for books which are exempt from VAT.

The first thing to do is to determine which tax rules apply to your store; you can then define them in Drupal Commerce.

Commerce Tax modules

Tax is part of Drupal Commerce core, so there is nothing new to download. Go to the module page and enable the following modules:

- Commerce Tax
- Commerce Tax UI

Setting up standard VAT

To start with, we will set up standard tax rates for our example store, which is based in the United Kingdom. Standard VAT is 20 percent here, but some food related items are taxed at a different rate.

From the toolbar, navigate to **Store | Configuration | Taxes**.

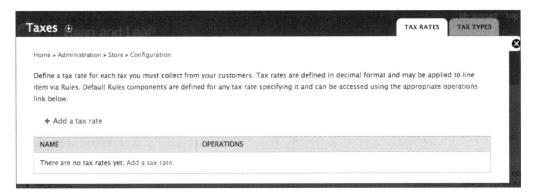

Click on **Add a tax rate**, set the type to be **VAT** and the rate to be 0.2 (20 percent), as shown in the following screenshot:

Food is rated at 0 percent; although this will obviously not result in a value other than zero, it is important to show a VAT exemption in your checkout.

Repeat the steps above to add a zero rate VAT band. You should now have two VAT rates set up.

VAT applied

Now if you view a product, you will see that the price has increased by 20 percent compared to the earlier one.

When you progress to the checkout, the VAT element is illustrated in the checkout summary.

At the moment, both the standard and zero rate tax apply but we will adjust this shortly.

Setting up a sales tax is an identical process; the only visual difference being that the customer sees the original price when browsing the store.

Determining which taxes apply

We mentioned earlier that the applicable taxes may change depending on the context of the products and order. At the moment, our tax rules apply to every product and as you will see in the previous screenshot, this is demonstrated by lines for both standard rate and zero rate tax.

Basic tax handling

In a simple scenario where the tax applied is not dependent on outside factors, such as location, you can simply edit the product and set the VAT code associated with the product. On the product edit screen you will see that the price field has a drop-down field next to it, where you can select one of the tax rates you created before, as shown in the following screenshot:

If you use this method, you should be entering the prices inclusive of VAT and should also note that the advanced tax calculations described in the following pages will not take effect.

Advanced tax handling

For more complex scenarios where there may be conditional taxes or multiple taxes being applied to a sale, the Commerce Tax module integrates with Rules allowing you to control the circumstances under which tax is applied to a product price.

Handling prices

Before we look at the rule, it is essential to understand how Drupal Commerce handles prices. Whenever a product price is displayed in the site catalog or cart, it is calculated dynamically by using rules. The only time that the price is locked is when the cart enters the checkout state.

The rules event, **Calculate Product Selling Price** is triggered whenever a selling price is displayed.

The Tax module has some predefined rules, which are created when you set up your tax rates. We set up two tax rates earlier and each one has a new rule set up.

Go to modules and enable the Product Pricing UI module, and we can see how this works. From the toolbar, navigate to **Store | Configuration | Product pricing rules**.

The last two rules in the list are created by the tax module; one for each type of tax. These rules are triggered whenever you are looking at a product with its price displayed on the site.

By default, the new rules have no conditions, which means they will apply to all products. If we add some conditions to the tax rules, we can be selective about which products will have tax applied.

When VAT is enabled and you edit a product, you may notice that the price field now has a drop-down menu where you can indicate whether the price you have entered already contains VAT at a certain rate.

Be careful if you use this option, as when set, it means that the tax rules do not apply (as they don't need to).

In our example, different products are taxed at different rates, so we need to come up with a way of distinguishing between them. The flexibility of Drupal and Rules means we could approach this in a number of different ways, so let's consider our options as follows:

Methods of determining applicable tax

Method	Pros	Cons
Create a new product variation type. Set up a condition to check the variation type and associate a variation type with a tax rate.	Simple rule condition.	Can't change a product's variation type after it has been created, so unforgiving of mistakes. May be overcomplicating things to have multiple product variant types if products are simple.
Add a VAT code field to the product variation type.	Allows the VAT code to be changed later.	If new taxes are added, the value would not be in the drop-down menu. Need to manually set VAT codes on all products.
Associate a Tax rate to a taxonomy.	Allows the VAT code to be changed later.	If new taxes are added, the value would not be in the drop-down menu. Need to manually set VAT code on all products.

How you approach this is a personal preference. I tend to use the method of creating a taxonomy due to the restriction on not being able to switch a product from one variation to another later.

Adding a VAT code taxonomy

Since products will not necessarily always have the same tax rate applying to them, for example, books are zero rated in the UK, we need a way of attaching a tax code to a product.

We could use a Drupal list type field, but it is always a good idea to use Taxonomy to manage lists of any type, so as to empower the eventual site administrator to make adjustments and additions. If we used a list field, then we would limit the developer's ability to edit.

Thus, create a new Taxonomy vocabulary, called Tax codes, containing the following two values:

- S, described as S for standard
- Z, described as Z for zero rated

Next, we need to attach the taxonomy to the Product entity, so that we have the ability to tag each product individually with a tax code, by using the following steps:

1. From the toolbar, navigate to **Store | Configuration | Product variation types**.
2. Click on **Manage fields** on the **Foodstuff** product. This will take you back to the familiar field management page.
3. Add a new **Term reference** field, called VAT code which references terms from our new **Tax code** vocabulary and use the **Select list** widget.
4. Set the field as **Required**, but also default to the **S** term for standard VAT. Note that we *do not* wish this to be an attributable field.
5. Finally then, you'll need to go back and edit each of your four existing product variations, so that they pick up the new **Tax code** field's default value of **S** for standard.
6. Clicking on **Save variation** on each will suffice.

Conditional tax rules

We will concentrate on the condition for applying the Standard tax rate, by using the following steps:

1. From the toolbar navigate to **Store | Configuration | Taxes**.
2. Click on **Configure component** next to Standard tax rate.
3. This will take you to the tax rule.

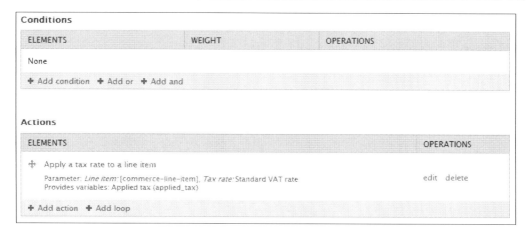

By default there are no conditions set, so this tax applies to all Products. However, we only want it to apply to line items containing a product with the **S** tax code.

The **Apply a Tax rate to a line** item action does exactly that; it actually applies tax calculations to line items, and while line items are very likely to be products, we cannot make that assumption.

So, in order to achieve our goal, we first need to look deeper into the line item, check whether it is a product, and if it is, then check the value of the **Tax code** field for that product and apply the standard, if appropriate.

Using Rules, we essentially need to ask the following questions:

- Is the line item a product?

    If so, then Rules will expose the fields of the product, so that we can check for the presence of a tax code field, then drill deeper and find out the value.

- What is the value of the **Tax code** field?

    The Rule interface is enormously powerful but by no means intuitive nor easy to explain in words and pictures, but here goes with a step-by-step guide.

Checking for the presence of a commerce product field

The following are the steps for checking the presence of a commerce product field:

1. Click on **Add a condition**.

2. Select the **Entity has field** option from the drop-down menu.

3. In the **Data selector** field, start typing commerce..., as shown in the following screenshot:

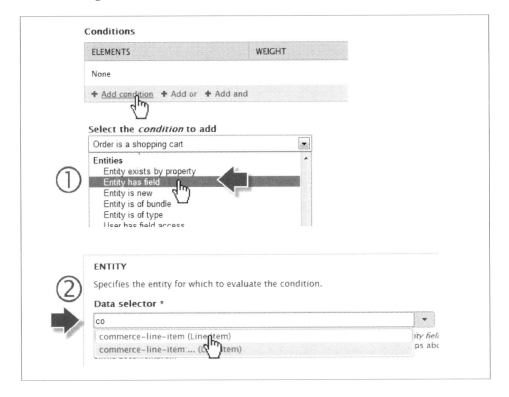

4. Select **commerce-line-item**.

5. In the **FIELD** drop-down menu, select **commerce_product**, as shown in the following screenshot:

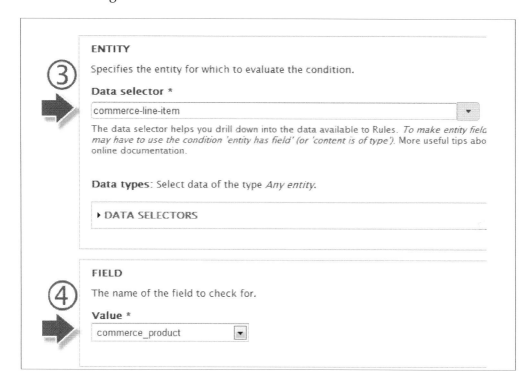

This condition makes sure that the line item we are looking at has a product associated with it and exposes the fields.

Checking for the presence of a tax code field

Next, we have to check that the referenced product variant type has a VAT code field associated with it, by using the following steps:

1. Click on **Add a condition**, as shown in the following screenshot:

2. Select the **Entity has field** option.

3. In the **Data selector** field, select **commerce-line-item:commerce-product**.

4. In the **FIELD** drop-down menu, select **field_tax_code**, as shown in the following screenshot:

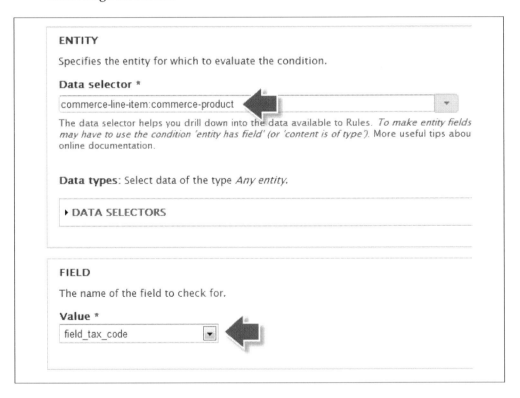

Checking for the value of a tax code field

Now that we have a VAT code field present, we can check the value.

We only want to apply this tax when the value is set to **S**.

The following are steps to check for the value of tax code field:

1. Click on **Add a condition**, as shown in the following screenshot:

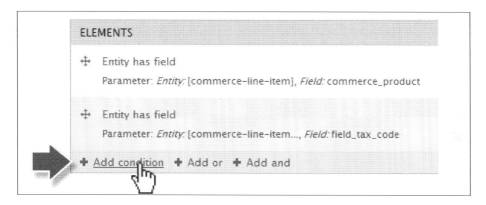

2. Choose **data comparison** in the **Data selector** field, select commerce-line-item:commerce-product:field-tax-code:name.

3. Note that we need to use the name property since our tax code is in fact a Taxonomy term.

4. Finally, select **Operator: equals**.

5. Select **Data Value** to **S**.

Repeating for zero rated tax

Now, do the same thing for your zero rate VAT rule, changing the data comparison value at the end.

Testing VAT conditions

Go to the product edit page and set the VAT code for one of your products.

Now, at the checkout you will only see the appropriate tax rate applied `cine £9 + £1.80 VAT = £10.80`, as shown in the following screenshot:

It would be better, however, if we could see the actual price breakdown, and we can achieve this simply by using an alternative field formatter within the cart view that provides the line item total as a breakdown.

Edit the view by clicking onto the cog icon in the top right-hand corner of the view, as shown in the following scareenshot:

Locate the line item **Total** field and click on it. Set the **Formatter** field to **Formatted amount with components**.

Apply the new setting and **Save** the view, and you should now see exactly what we are looking for.

Summary

You now have the ability to set different tax rates for different products. Setting up sales tax for the USA follows exactly the same principles.

You may also want to investigate other tax modules for conditional charging of VAT based on the shipping country.

9
Managing Orders

We have given our customers everything that they need to place an order in our store; now we need to process the orders coming in.

Configuring the back office

Firstly, enable the Commerce BackOffice Order module.

This has dependencies on the following modules which you will need to install as well:

- http://drupal.org/project/date
- http://drupal.org/project/eva

From the toolbar, navigate to **Store | Orders**.

The order screen allows you to search for an order by status, date, customer name, e-mail address, or order ID.

You can either click on **Quick edit**, to expand the order on the same screen, as shown in the following screenshot, or you can click edit to open the full order:

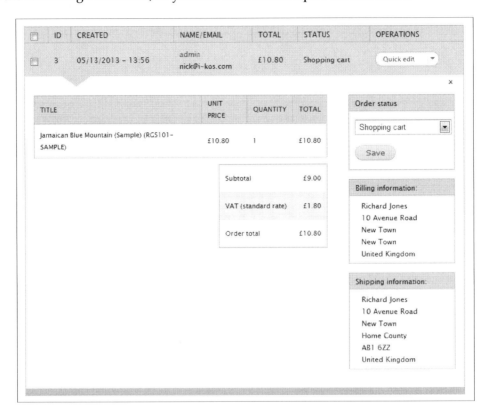

Default order states and status codes

The site we have built so far will provide the following order status codes:

State	Status
Shopping cart	Shopping Cart
Checkout	Checkout: Checkout
Checkout	Checkout: Shipping
Checkout	Checkout: Review
Checkout	Checkout: Payment

State	Status
Checkout	Checkout: Complete
Pending	Pending
Pending	Processing
Completed	Completed

When you view your orders, you can determine the progress that the customer has made through the checkout process.

When a customer has paid in full for an order, the status will be updated to **Pending: Pending**. This is the default behavior for Drupal Commerce, but note that you may want to change this for certain types of products, where there is no physical fulfillment of the order (for example, membership or digital products).

Simple convention for the use of status codes

The way that you use the status codes depends on how you model your order fulfillment process.

When setting up a simple status code, I define the status codes as follows:

Status Code	Description
Cart / Checkout States	Customer is still shopping and has not yet completed the payment process.
Pending: Pending	Payment received for the order, but no fulfillment action has yet started.
Pending: Processing	Order is being handled ready for delivery. For example, in stores for picking.
Completed: Completed	Order has been collected by courier and is in transit.

The order status can be changed in the quick edit or full edit screens.

Viewing payment transactions

In the edit drop-down menu of the order line, you can also select the **Payment** menu, as shown in the following screenshot:

What you see on the payments screen is determined by the functionality of the Payment gateway module that you have selected. In the following screen shot, I have temporarily enabled the **Example payment** method and used that for the order. This gives me the ability to view the details of the transaction.

By contrast, the SagePay integration module provides extensive data about the transaction and also allows you to perform secondary transactions, such as refunds and voids. These functions are presented as operations in the transaction list.

The functionality offered by the Payment gateway modules varies depending on how many of the available hooks the module developer has implemented. If you want to do more advanced transaction handling, such as repeating payments, refunds, or voids, it is worth checking out the capabilities of the payment gateway modules before you make the final choice of gateway to use.

Summary

If a Drupal Commerce module exists for the payment gateway that you want to integrate with, the process is very easy. Check `drupal.org`, or `drupalcommerce. org`, to see if your gateway is supported.

If the payment gateway you need does not have a module listed on `drupal.org`, you can create one using the API documentation from the gateway provider. However, this is no small undertaking and not a topic for a getting started book!

10
Discounts and Coupons

The world of e-commerce is a competitive place and there are often requirements to change the selling prices of products and create special offers for customers. These come in many guises; some more complex than others.

In this chapter, we will review the different techniques for offering discounts and coupons, and discuss the opportunities and limitations of each.

Site-wide discounts

In our first scenario, we will offer 10 percent off on all of our selling prices throughout the site.

To achieve this, we can create a pricing rule similar to those used earlier for calculating taxes. From the toolbar, navigate to **Store | Configuration | Product pricing rules**. Click on **Add pricing rule**.

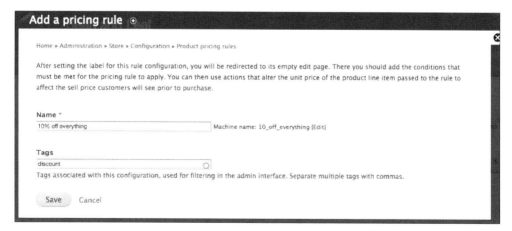

Add an action to the new rule, named **Multiply Unit Price by Some Amount**.

Multiplying the unit price by 0.9 is the same as a 10 percent discount.

The final price is made up of multiple components. We can either use this rule to override the base price or we can add the discount as a separate component.

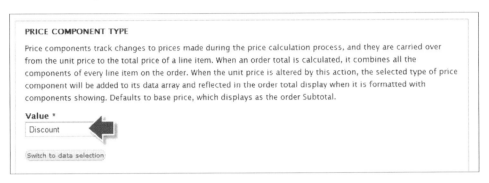

If the calculation leads to a partial currency unit, we can determine what action to take. The default is **Round the half up**, but different countries have different rules of how this should apply.

Our product which was originally **£9** is now shown as £8.10 +VAT.

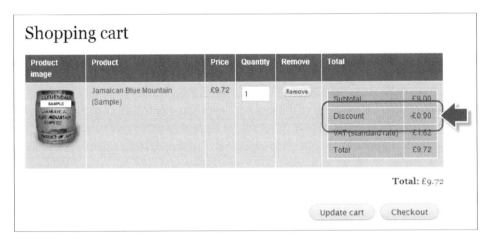

Extra price discount format

You can add in some other useful price formatters using the Commerce Extra Price Formatters module, available at http://drupal.org/project/commerce_extra_price_formatters.

This module allows you to control how the prices are displayed to the customer. From the toolbar, navigate to **Store | Configuration | Product variation types**.

Click on **manage display** on the **Product variation type** field.

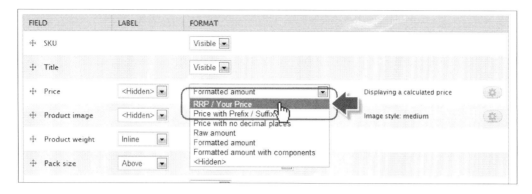

The default formatter for the price is **Formatted Amount,** but now that you have installed the new module, you will see other available options.

Select **RRP / Your Price**, and then click on the gear icon to get to the settings.

You can now set some parameters for how you would like the product price to be displayed. For now, accept the defaults and then go back to the product page.

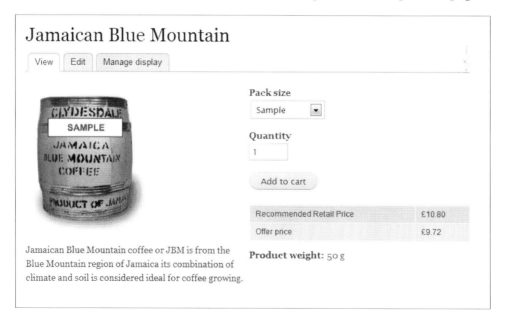

Limiting the discounts to a date range

If we want these special promotional prices to apply for a limited time only, we can add conditions to our rule. To achieve our goal, we are going to check the current date, that is the date at the moment a shopper looks at a product, to see if it is within a given date range.

We are going to add a check, such that the offer is only available in July.

Creating your rule

The following are the steps for creating your rule:

1. From the toolbar navigate to **Store | Configuration | Product pricing rules**.

2. Edit the 10 percent of everything rule. Also, add a condition.

3. Choose **Data comparison**.

4. Now, we are going to compare the current date to make sure that we are not still in June.

5. Type `site` in the selection box and pick off **site:current-date** (that is, without the trailing dots).

6. Click on **Continue** and then perform the check to see if June has passed.

7. Since we want to compare the current date to an absolute value of June 30, rather than comparing it to the value of some other property or field, we should now switch this section of the UI to **direct input mode**, so we can enter our fixed value. Note that there are two input modes, namely direct input and data selection. If you see **Switch to data selection**, then you are already in direct input mode.

8. You can now enter the absolute date to compare with and change the operator value to **is greater than**.

9. Save the condition and you should see it added to your Rule.

+ Data comparison

Parameter: *Data to compare:* [site:current-date], *Operator:* is greater than, *Data value:* 06/30/2013 - 00:00   edit delete

---

10. Next, using the same method, add the check for the beginning of August, changing the operator to **is lower than**.

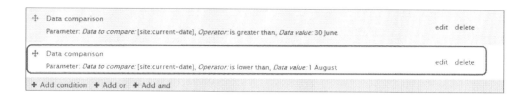

Testing your rule

If you visit the store at any time other than in July, the original price should apply.

You can test your new rule by temporarily altering the clock on your local machine, so that your Drupal site thinks the date is somewhere in July.

Coupons

Coupons or offer codes are a popular way of offering discounts to selected customers or via advertising.

To use Coupons in Drupal Commerce, we need to install some new modules:

* `http://drupal.org/project/commerce_coupon`
* `http://drupal.org/project/commerce_coupon_fixed_amount`
* `http://drupal.org/project/commerce_coupon_pct`
* `http://drupal.org/project/entityreference`

Enable the following modules:

* Commerce Coupon
* Commerce Coupon Fixed Amount
* Commerce Coupon Percentage Amount
* Commerce Coupon UI
* Entity Reference

You will now have an extra menu in your store settings, named **Coupons**.

Fixed discount on your order

Our first example is to give a customer £10 off their order, by using the following steps:

1. Click on **Create coupon** and you will be presented with a choice of creating a fixed price coupon or a percentage coupon.

2. Click on **Create Fixed coupon**.

3. Enter the £10 value and OFFER as an offer code, as shown in the following screenshot:

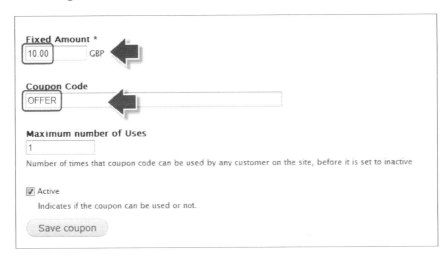

4. Now that the coupon module has been enabled, an extra checkout pane will be visible, as shown in the following screenshot:

You can change the position of the coupon pane within the checkout process, as described in *Chapter 6, Checkout*.

When the customer redeems their coupon, a new line is added to the order, as shown in the following screenshot:

Adding an expiry date to a coupon

If we want a coupon to only be valid for a certain time, we can use rules to add an expiry date. To do this, first we need to alter the coupon to add an expiry date field.

1. From the toolbar, navigate to **Store | Coupons**.
2. Then click on the **Coupon types** tab.
3. Click on **manage fields** on the **Fixed coupon field**.
4. Now, add a new field called `Expiry date`, setting the **Type** field to **Date** and the **WIDGET** to **Popup Calendar**.
5. Accept the defaults on the field settings page and click on **Save field settings**.
6. Your field will now apply to all existing fixed coupons and any that you build in the future.

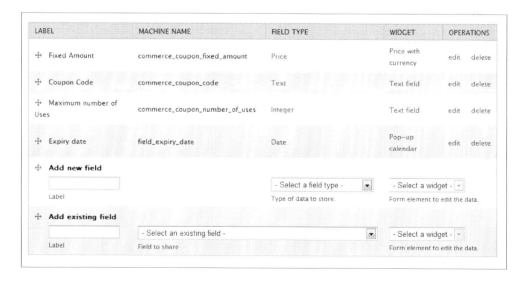

7. If you now go back and edit the coupon we used earlier, you will see the new field in place.

8. The expiry date can now be set to a specific date and time.

9. We now need to set up a rule to check if the coupon has expired. There is a Rule event triggered, called **Validate a Coupon**, whenever the customer attempts to enter a coupon code. This Rule checks that the number of uses has not exceeded the set value for each coupon by checking the **Maximum number of Uses** field.

10. We will now build a similar rule that checks the value of the new **Expiry date** field.

11. From the toolbar, navigate to **Configuration | Workflow | Rules**.

12. Add a new rule.

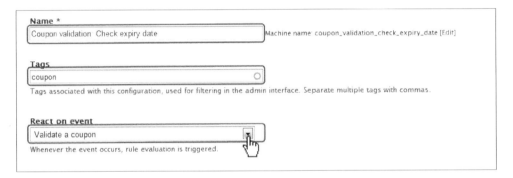

13. Next, add a condition to check for the presence of the **Expiry date** field using **Entity has field**.

14. For the data selector **coupon**, look for the **Expiry date** field.

15. Save this condition.

16. Now that we have established the existence of the **Expiry date** field, we can drill into it to pick up the actual value.

17. Add another condition; this time a data comparison with the coupon as the data selector.

18. Click on **Continue** and pick off the **Expiry date** field from the **Coupon** entity.
19. Continue and compare the value of the field.

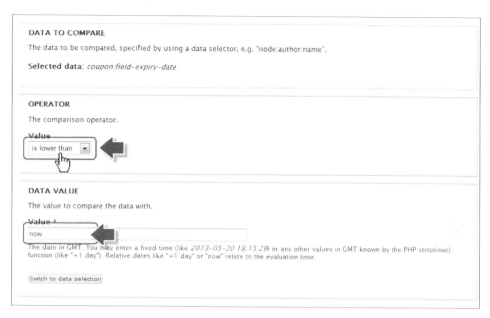

This means the rule actions will trigger if the coupon has an expiry date field and the value of the date is before the current time.

Add an action to the Rule: **Set coupon as invalid**.

We want to do it this way round as the coupon is assumed to be valid unless we say otherwise. We are looking to determine the negative condition, so we can declare the coupon as invalid.

Summary

Discounts and coupons are very powerful in Drupal Commerce, but as you can see, the setting up of rules is complex and may be intimidating at first. However, by following these steps, you can define coupons and offers that are reusable so that the next ones you set up are straight forward.

Index

store currency
  setting up 33
subscriptions
  selling 25
Subsite field 17

T

tax
  applicable tax determining, process 101
  handling, advanced 99
  handling, basics 99
  rates 95
  rules, conditional 102
  types 95
tax code field
  presence, checking 105, 106
  value, checking 107
taxes 28
tax modules 96
taxonomy
  terms, adding 46, 47
taxonomy vocabulary 26
tickets
  selling 24
token module
  about 10
  URL 10
Tracking Code 93

U

unique ID (uid) 10
URL path settings 54
user 7
user experience 31

V

Validate a Coupon 124
Value added Tax. *See* VAT
variable pricing 27
VAT
  about 28, 95
  applicable tax determining, methods 101
  code field, adding 101, 102
  conditional tax rules 102
  conditions, testing 107, 108
  in checkout summary 98
  prices, handling 99
  proces, handling 100
  setting up 96, 97
  tax handling, advanced 99
  tax handling, basic 99
VAT code field
  adding 101, 102
views module
  about 9
  URL 9

W

Web Payments Standard (WPS) payment
  method 78

Thank you for buying
Getting Started with Drupal Commerce

About Packt Publishing

Packt, pronounced 'packed', published its first book "*Mastering phpMyAdmin for Effective MySQL Management*" in April 2004 and subsequently continued to specialize in publishing highly focused books on specific technologies and solutions.

Our books and publications share the experiences of your fellow IT professionals in adapting and customizing today's systems, applications, and frameworks. Our solution based books give you the knowledge and power to customize the software and technologies you're using to get the job done. Packt books are more specific and less general than the IT books you have seen in the past. Our unique business model allows us to bring you more focused information, giving you more of what you need to know, and less of what you don't.

Packt is a modern, yet unique publishing company, which focuses on producing quality, cutting-edge books for communities of developers, administrators, and newbies alike. For more information, please visit our website: www.packtpub.com.

About Packt Open Source

In 2010, Packt launched two new brands, Packt Open Source and Packt Enterprise, in order to continue its focus on specialization. This book is part of the Packt Open Source brand, home to books published on software built around Open Source licences, and offering information to anybody from advanced developers to budding web designers. The Open Source brand also runs Packt's Open Source Royalty Scheme, by which Packt gives a royalty to each Open Source project about whose software a book is sold.

Writing for Packt

We welcome all inquiries from people who are interested in authoring. Book proposals should be sent to author@packtpub.com. If your book idea is still at an early stage and you would like to discuss it first before writing a formal book proposal, contact us; one of our commissioning editors will get in touch with you.

We're not just looking for published authors; if you have strong technical skills but no writing experience, our experienced editors can help you develop a writing career, or simply get some additional reward for your expertise.

Building E-commerce Sites with Drupal Commerce Cookbook

ISBN: 978-1-78216-122-6   Paperback: 206 pages

Over 50 recipes to help you build engaging, responsive E-commerce sites with Drupal Commerce

1. Learn how to build attractive eCommerce sites with Drupal Commerce

2. Customise your Drupal Commerce store for maximum impact

3. Reviewed by the creators of Drupal Commerce: The CommerceGuys

Drupal 7 Business Solutions

ISBN: 978-1-84951-664-8   Paperback: 378 pages

Build powerful website features for your business

1. Build a Drupal 7 powered website for your business rapidly

2. Add blogs, news, e-commerce, image galleries, maps, surveys, polls, and forums to your website to beat competition

3. Complete example of a real world site with clear explanation

Please check **www.PacktPub.com** for information on our titles

Drupal 7 Development by Example Beginner's Guide

ISBN: 978-1-84951-680-8   Paperback: 366 pages

Follow the creation of Drupal website to learn, by example, the key concepts of Drupal 7 development and HTML5

1. A hands-on, example-driven guide to programming Drupal websites

2. Discover a number of new features for Drupal 7 through practical and interesting examples while building a fully functional recipe sharing website

3. Learn about web content management, multi-media integration, and e-commerce in Drupal 7

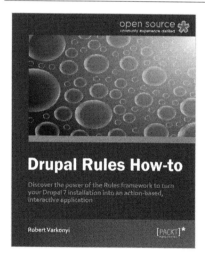

Drupal Rules How-to

ISBN: 978-1-84951-998-4   Paperback: 74 pages

Discover the power of the Rules framework to turn your Drupal 7 installation into an action-based, interactive application

1. Learn something new in an Instant! A short, fast, focused guide delivering immediate results.

2. Leverage the power of Rules and Views Bulk Operations

3. Re-use configurations using Components

4. Create your own Events, Conditions and Actions.

Please check **www.PacktPub.com** for information on our titles

Printed in Great Britain
by Amazon